Streetsmarts

A TEENAGER'S SAFETY GUIDE

Streetsmarts

JANE GOLDMAN

This American edition of STREETSMARTS, first published in the United Kingdom in 1995 as SUSSED AND STREETWISE, is published by arrangement with Piccadilly Press Limited, London, England.

All inquiries should be addressed to:
Barron's Educational Series, Inc.
250 Wireless Boulevard
Hauppauge, NY 11788-3917

Library of Congress Catalog Card No. 96-2497
International Standard Book No. 0-8120-9762-9

Library of Congress Cataloging-in-Publication Data

Goldman, Jane, 1970–
Streetsmarts : a teenager's safety guide / Jane Goldman.
p. cm.
Includes index.
ISBN 0-8120-9762-9
1. Teenagers—United States—Life skills guides. 2. Teenagers—United States—Conduct of life. I. Title.
HQ796.G595 1996
646.7'00835—dc20 96-2497
CIP

PRINTED IN THE UNITED STATES OF AMERICA

Jane Goldman is a young writer who lives in North London with her husband and two children. She worked for a number of years on *Just Seventeen* magazine before turning freelance. She has written three other books; *Thirteensomething, Sex: How? Why? What?*, and *For Weddings, A Funeral and When You Can't Flush the Loo.*

Contents

OUT AND ABOUT 41

GETTING FROM A TO B—TRANSPORTATION 56

AT HOME 73

AT SCHOOL 97

COPING WITH CRIME 118

Introduction

In case you were wondering, this book is not just for girls. Although we tend to think of girls and women as being more vulnerable than boys and men, this is misleading. Statistics show that with many types of crime (mugging, for instance), males are actually more likely to be victims.

Sadly, no one can take safety for granted. But everyone—male or female, old or young, weak or strong—can benefit from being more aware about avoiding dangerous situations, and knowing what to do if they find themselves threatened.

The commonsense advice in this book applies to *everybody*. And remember: This is the 90s. Everyone knows that girls are no longer expected to be the meek, powerless creatures in need of protection that they once were. But just as that silly old stereotype is dead, so are the rules that boys have to be macho, tough, and fearless—which is just as much nonsense. We've all got to forget how we're *supposed* to be, and concentrate on the far more important business of being aware, confident, and determined in our beliefs that we deserve to enjoy life without coming up against fear and danger.

Thinking about safety doesn't mean you're paranoid. Avoiding risks doesn't make you a wimp. Taking precautions doesn't mark you as a scaredy-cat. And if you've figured all that out for yourself already, congratulations—you've taken the first and most important step toward becoming truly streetsmart.

Chapter

Parties and Nights on the Town 1

After all the hard work you put in at school, you deserve to get out of the house, relax, and have a good time with your friends, and it would be silly to let paranoia dampen your fun. But it would be even sillier to refuse to think about safety when you're going out because you can't be bothered, or because you don't want to spoil your happy mood.

DECIDING WHAT TO WEAR

"I was just about to leave for the party when my mom and dad threw a fit about these little shorts I was wearing. I tried to tell them that I wasn't wearing them to look sexy, it was just the fashion, but my dad said 'try explaining that to a rapist.' In the end I got so upset that I changed into jeans, even though I still thought deep down that they were talking nonsense."

Daisy, 15

No matter what some parents (and, alarmingly, some insensitive and idiotic judges) might say, a girl who goes out wearing something that shows off her figure is not "asking for it." She does not deserve to be raped or attacked any more than a girl who goes out wearing a floor-length potato sack. And there is no proof that keeping yourself covered up or looking dowdy makes you safer.

Of course, if you go out wearing something particularly sexy and eye-catching, you might get some unwanted attention from men, but it's most likely to be wolf whistles and crude comments (see Chapter Three). That's not to say that it *couldn't* be worse, but it's far more important to concentrate on the main issue: avoiding dangerous situations where an attack is possible.

However, if you're going to be out on the streets or on public transportation it *is* worth thinking about whether your clothes are going to hamper you in any way. It's a horrible thought, but what if you had to run to get away from someone? Are your heels too high or uncomfortable? Are your clothes too tight? Use common sense. If you're getting a lift to and from where you're going, wear whatever you fancy. If not, go for comfortable footwear and clothes you can move freely in. Don't forget that you can always throw some fancier stuff in a bag and change when you arrive.

ALCOHOL

"I don't drink alcohol because I don't like the taste of it, but I know a few people my age who do. I can't understand people who drink because they want to look cool. At the parties I've been to it's always the drunk ones who end up doing the most uncool, embarrassing things!"

Ben, 14

"It seemed like one minute I was having a great time, and the next the whole room was spinning around and around... The worst thing was definitely the next day,

when my mom made me phone my friend's mom to say sorry for being sick on their carpet."

Debbie, 14

"I always thought that losing my virginity would be this great, important experience. As it was, all I can really remember is getting drunk at the party, then waking up on a pile of coats feeling like death warmed over and realizing that my panties and leggings were around my ankles and the guy I'd been talking to all night was lying next to me. I hadn't even liked him."

Claire, 16

Before I say anything else, I've got to mention that it's against the law for people to sell you booze or let you drink it in their home or a public place if you're under twenty-one. That said, if you go to a party where there is alcohol, it's up to you to decide whether you're going to drink or not—so use common sense. You should never drink alcohol for stupid reasons: because you're afraid that turning it down will make you look babyish, because your friends are encouraging you, because everyone else is boozing and you don't want to be left out. If you feel that you want to drink alcohol, here are two important facts to bear in mind:

• Alcohol can make you behave in ways that you wouldn't normally behave. That could mean getting into an argument, blurting out your best friend's deepest darkest secret, telling someone else's boyfriend that you've always liked him, making out with somebody disgusting, or jumping on the table and doing an enthusiastic impression of a bar room singer. It could also mean getting into a make-out session that ends up going a lot further than you feel comfortable about the next day. If you're drunk, you might also take risks getting home—it's amazing how having a little walk through dark deserted streets doesn't seem particularly scary or dangerous when you're sloshed. And of course, when your judgment is impaired, it also means that you might not be able to judge when to *stop* drinking, and you could just keep on chugging until you get seriously ill, pass out, or do something really, really stupid—like fall out of a window, walk under a car, or have unprotected sex.

• Alcohol can make you wildly ill. You could just feel queasy and dizzy and desperate to lie down, which would certainly put an end to any fun at the party. It's not unlikely that you might actually upchuck, too—again, not much of a laugh, and not very sociable either (especially if you don't make it to the bathroom). You could also fall asleep in an alcohol-induced stupor, which (a) makes you look pretty stupid; (b) makes it a bit difficult to get home; (c) makes you a big pain in the butt for your friends, who have to look after you; and (d) leaves you with a huge headache the next day.

However, things can also get pretty serious. If you fall asleep and then throw up, which is quite possible, you could choke to death on your own vomit. It's also possible to get full-blown alcohol poisoning—a very serious condition that requires a visit to a hospital, and, if you're extremely unlucky, can kill you.

If you do decide to drink, always follow these safety hints:

• Don't drink too much. One small alcoholic drink, possibly two, spaced well apart, is a sensible limit. It takes different amounts of alcohol to make people tipsy or ill (gender, height, size, metabolism, genes, and what you've had to eat that day all play a part). So never try to keep up with anyone else—listen to your body and let it tell you when you've had enough.

• Stick to drinking just one kind of alcohol. Mixing drinks can make you drunker and sicker than sticking to one kind, and it'll all happen that much more quickly. If you're not sure, the different alcohol groups are:

1) Beer.

2) White wine, rosé wine, sparkling wine, and champagne.

3) Red wine and port.

4) Hard liquor or spirits—vodka, gin, whiskey, rum, brandy, tequila. Southern Comfort and bourbon are different kinds of whiskey, and Malibu contains rum, so it also counts as a spirit.

5) Liqueurs—there are loads of different kinds. Some common ones are Baileys, Cointreau, crème de menthe, cherry brandy, and advocaat. A "snowball" is a cocktail made with advocaat (which is sometimes sold ready-made in little bottles).

• Spirits and liqueurs are far stronger drinks than beer, cider, or wine, and will make you drunk or sick far more quickly if you drink a lot of them.

• Home-brewed beer or wine is often ridiculously strong, so if any is available, you should either steer clear or drink only a very little. Fortunately, home brews usually taste and smell astonishingly like urine, so this isn't too difficult.

• Beware of fruit punches at parties—they're usually far more alcoholic than they taste, and therefore it's quite easy to drink too much before you even realize it. Similarly, if you're drinking an alcoholic drink mixed with something else, either pour the drink yourself or guide the person making it for you so that you know exactly how much alcohol is going in.

• If you haven't eaten anything for a while, alcohol will take effect much more quickly, and you'll be more likely to feel ill.

• Drink slowly, and once you've had one drink, don't rush to have another right away. Alcohol takes a few minutes to have an effect, and it's all too easy to be feeling fine one minute and grab another drink, only to find that the effect of the two drinks put together knocks you sideways.

• Always keep track of how much you've had to drink—it can get out of control very quickly.

• If you're drinking alcohol, always drink lots and lots of nonalcoholic liquid, preferably water, as well. It dilutes the alcohol, and helps prevent dehydration, so it can help a bit in stopping you from getting too drunk or too ill.

• If you start to feel slightly peculiar—dizzy, sick, whatever—stop drinking alcohol right away and start downing water.

• If you feel really sick after drinking alcohol, it's always better to throw up. It's your body's way of getting the alcohol out of your system, and can prevent alcohol poisoning.

• Even if you only drink a little, the chances are that you're going to feel really, really vile the following morning. For this reason, it's incredibly stupid to drink if you've got to get up early or do something important the next day. Drinking lots of water before you go to bed, and getting as much sleep as you can is the best way to make sure that you're not totally wiped out.

DRUGS

"My dad told me that he tried pot when he was young, and that he didn't mind if I tried it one day, as long as I never tried any hard drugs. I think that was a much better thing to tell me than what some of my friends' parents say to them, which is that they shouldn't ever try drugs at all. I mean, don't they know that the more they tell you not to do something, the more you want to do it? I'm lucky because my dad is really cool and he really understands what teenagers are like."

David, 13

"I would definitely never try acid or anything like that because my sister tried it and had a bad trip. Her friends brought her home, and she was screaming that it was raining blood and everybody had turned into zombies. She thought my mom and I were zombies too. We took her to the hospital, and they strapped her on a gurney and said there was nothing you could do except wait for

it to wear off. We were all there for six hours, with her going crazy the whole time. It was the worst six hours of my entire life."

Helen, 15

"My aunt is just a bit older than me and she really turned me off taking drugs by telling me about this girl she knew who took something at a party—I'm not sure what it was—and she had a really bad reaction to it. She was okay at the time, but the next day she broke out in this kind of acne, all over her face and chest and arms everywhere. She didn't want to go to the doctor because she didn't want to tell him about the drugs, and it took months to go away."

Lara, 17

I'm sure you don't need me to tell you that drugs are illegal. I'm sure you also don't need me to tell you that having a drug habit can ruin your entire life. What you may not know, though, is that there are very big risks involved even in trying stuff just once. For instance, you should know that:

• All drugs are addictive. Some are strongly physically addictive—like crack, heroin, and cocaine. In other words, once you've taken them once or twice, your body tells you in all sorts of unpleasant ways that it needs some more, pronto. Other drugs might be less physically addictive, but they're still addictive in that if you try them once and enjoy it, you're going to be tempted to do it again.

• Doing drugs is an unpredictable business. So often,

you hear terrible, sad stories of people who sniff a solvent or aerosol, have a bad reaction to it, and drop dead right there while all their friends look on helplessly. You never know how your body is going to react to any kind of drug. And even if you try something once and are fine, it doesn't necessarily mean that you'll be okay if you do it again.

• Hallucinogenic drugs, like magic mushrooms and LSD (acid), are also very unpredictable in the effect they can have on you. When you take them, they change the whole way your brain works, and they make you see, hear, and think strange things. But you never know from one time to the next whether those things are going to be nice or terrifying.

Another risk you take with many drugs, such as speed, cocaine, heroin, and ecstasy, is that you just don't know what's in them. The money-grabbing scumbags who sell them make their cash by buying the drug, then adding other stuff to it so that they can sell it off in as many units as possible. If you're lucky, this just means that you get suckered into paying a ridiculous amount of money for what is basically a bunch of harmless powder—baby laxative, crushed-up pills, whatever—and a tiny bit of the drug you thought you were getting. If you're unlucky, it can mean that you're stuffing your body with awful, dangerous things like household cleaning powder and other poisons. People have ended up hospitalized or dead because of this sort of thing. Even if you escape without serious effect, you could have a terrible allergic reaction.

All told, drugs just aren't worth the risk. Remember:

• If you can't have a good time without taking drugs, you've got a big problem.

• If your friends want to try drugs, it's worth making a big effort to dissuade them. Otherwise, let them do it—you can feel proud that you're mature enough to make your own choices and protect your health.

• If your friends hassle you into trying drugs, it's time to look for a new crowd to hang out with. Real friends don't put their friends under pressure about *anything*.

This advice also goes for smoking. Nicotine is a legal drug (although you're not allowed to buy cigarettes under the age of 18), but it's still a drug—a very addictive one too—and still very bad for you. Remember that most people who smoke started in their teens, and wish that they hadn't. If you don't start now, the chances are that you never will.

THE OPPOSITE SEX

"Most of the boys at the party were much older, and one of them made a beeline for me right away. I really liked him and we chatted and then we started making out. He said we should sneak off to one of the bedrooms and I didn't even think about it really. It was fine until he started sticking his hand up my top and undoing my jeans and all that. He got really annoyed when I tried to stop him. He did stop, though, thank god. He said, 'You're lucky I'm such a nice guy,' and stormed off. I was

really upset because I liked him, but thinking about it later, it gave me the creeps. It could have been much worse, and no one would have been able to hear me shout for help over the music."

Naomi, 15

If you're going to a party where there will be members of the opposite sex, it doesn't necessarily mean that there is going to be making out going on, and if there is, it's probably not going to lead to any problems. However, it pays to be aware that things can occasionally go too far. Remember that you always have the right to say no to something you don't want to do. There is no such thing as "leading someone on" or being a "tease" or—that horrible phrase again—"asking for it." With any luck, the people you hang out with will know and respect these facts. But be wise: sneaking off to a bedroom for privacy sends out the message that you're planning to do something that's too raunchy to do in front of everyone else. Of course, that still doesn't give anyone the right to force you into something you don't want to do, but it's not a good idea to give people mixed signals. Most importantly, though, you should bear in mind that being in a room alone with someone—particularly someone who is physically bigger than you and all fired up—is a potentially dangerous situation that is best avoided unless you know and trust that person 100 percent. For more on this subject, see Chapter Two.

GETTING HOME

"My dad once picked me up from a party wearing his pajamas, slippers, and old bathrobe with cat poo stains

on it. That was ten years ago and I think I still haven't fully recovered from the humiliation. Mind you, there were quite a few times when I was standing around nervously waiting for the night bus that my dad would have been the most welcome sight in the world—poo-stained bathrobe and all—and to hell with what my friends thought."

Jane Goldman (me), 24

There are so many things to think about when you're going out—what to wear, how you're going to get there, what you're going to do—that it's not really surprising if you don't give much thought to how you're going to get home. This can be a fatal mistake to make. We all know how dangerous it can be to be stranded in the dark, especially if you're not sure where you are or how to get back, and yet so many people find themselves in that situation so often.

Ideally, planning how you're going to get home should be something you do automatically, every time you go out. With all that other stuff on your mind, it can be a hard habit to get into, but it's very important that you do. At best, being stranded is annoying, confusing, and a bit scary. At worst, it could mean being followed, threatened, or attacked. Either way, it's a horrible way to end an otherwise great evening out—and if you actually get attacked, that's going to be putting it mildly!

Once you're in the habit of planning your return journeys, you've taken a big step on the road to safety. But *how* you choose to travel is obviously very important too. You need to be especially careful getting around alone at night. I'm sure we all agree that this is a stupid, terrible state of affairs, and that *everybody* should have the right to walk around freely or wait for a bus or train at any time of the day or night without fear of anything bad happening to them, but that's just the way things are, unfortunately. "Standing up for your rights" by walking home on your own or waiting alone at a deserted bus stop in the middle of the night isn't going to change a thing. The sad fact is that there are sick people out there who don't respect those rights, and they are not going to see you and think: "Wow, now *there's* someone who isn't prepared to accept the unfair rules of modern society. I suppose I'd better not attack her, then. Ho hum. Perhaps I'll go home and have a nice cup of hot chocolate instead."

Let's check out all the ways you can get home after a night out:

By car

• Getting picked up by your parents.

Some people find this hideously embarrassing, especially if they've been at a party, and their mom or dad decides to—cringe—come in. The fact is, though, that this is definitely one of the safest ways to get home, so either grin and bear it (*everyone* has parents—it's really not *that* embarrassing), or arrange beforehand that you'll come outside at a specific time. If you're not sure when the party will finish, or you're worried about interrupting a particularly fabulous chat/dance/necking session, you could agree on a rough pick-up time with your folks, but arrange that you'll call home to let them know when you're ready to be picked up.

• Getting a ride home with someone else's parents. This is great because it means you have all the safety and none of the embarrassment. It's also great for your parents, because they don't have to heave themselves out of bed every time you go out.

If you often go out with the same friend, and that friend doesn't live too far from you, perhaps your parents and theirs could come to an arrangement that they'll take turns picking you both up and dropping you both home.

• Getting a ride home with anyone else. You should only get into someone's car if you're sure that you're going to be safe. Don't accept rides from people you don't know or trust (particularly if you're going to be the only passenger), from people who have been drinking, or from very young drivers who may not be too skilled behind the wheel in the dark (or may not even have a license yet and may be driving illegally). If you're certain that the person offering you a lift is trustworthy, sober, and able to drive, the final thing to check, before you get in the car, is whether they're prepared to take you all the way to your front door. There's no sense in accepting a ride if you're going to get thrown out before you get home because the driver doesn't want to go out of his or her way. That leaves you with no choice but to walk the rest of the way if you're close to home, or search around for a bus or phone if you're not—basically, you'll be in a far more dangerous position than if you hadn't gotten the lift in the first place.

For more essential info on getting rides, see Chapter Four.

By taxi

On the whole, a taxi is a reliable, safe way to travel because it takes you from door to door. There are some important rules and warnings to follow, though—see Chapter Four.

By public transportation

Traveling alone at night by public transportation can be fairly risky.

For a start, it often means a long walk, maybe through a deserted area, to get home once you're off the bus or train. And then there's the fact that you often get a lot of drunk people traveling home late at night on public transportation. This doesn't necessarily make them dangerous, but, as we stated before, being drunk makes people behave in ways they wouldn't normally—so there's more chance that people are going to talk to you, make comments, etc., which can be pretty unsettling.

It's a very good idea to travel with someone else, so if you've got a friend who is going out with you and lives nearby it's a good idea to plan on traveling home together. Better still, arrange for your friend to spend the night with you, or vice versa, so that you've both got company from door to door.

If you need to travel home on public transportation alone, make sure that you plan well ahead, finding out exactly where the nearest bus stop or train station is, how to get there directly, whether you'll need to change buses or trains, and what times the buses or trains run (or are supposed to run!).

Often the most dangerous aspect of traveling by public

transportation is the walking you have to do to get to or from the stop or station, and the time you have to spend standing around waiting. For more info, see below, and Chapters Three and Four.

Walking home

As I said earlier, it *is* outrageous that it's not safe to walk the streets at night. If walking home after you've been out seems like your best option—or your only option—try to persuade someone else to walk you home.

See Chapter Three for more safety hints on getting around on foot.

Let's recap...

The essential getting-home safety rules

- Always plan how you're going to get home ahead of time.

- If your travel plans include walking or taking public transportation at night, try to travel with a friend, rather than alone.

- Always make sure that you have a handful of change in your pocket at the end of the night—enough for your bus or train fare or to make a phone call. If you can afford it, it's a good idea to carry enough money to pay for a taxi—just in case.

- If you find yourself stranded, it's far better to phone your parents and ask them for help, even if you're sure they'll be angry. Think about it: being woken up by a call from you late at night is preferable to getting a phone call from the police later on saying that you're in the hospital... Or worse.

- Try to make phone calls from busy places rather than from pay phones on the street, especially when it's dark and you'd have to hang around waiting to be picked up. Garages, restaurants, cafes, pubs, and hotels are always a good bet. If there is a problem with going into a pub because you're under age, ask to see the manager and explain that you're stranded and you just want to use the phone.

- Don't forget that there are ways to get around having no money. You can make a collect call to your home through the operator (dial 0). The operator will ask for your name and will tell whoever answers the phone that it is you calling.

- If you know that you have some money at home, you can call or catch a taxi and get them to take you home, then run in and get the cash to pay them. Although you are not legally supposed to ride in a cab unless you have the money to pay for it on you, the driver is bound to be understanding if you're stranded. If he doesn't look like the sympathetic type, though, remember that you don't have to tell him that you don't have the money until you get home anyway.

ON VACATION

If you're lucky enough to be invited to a party while you're on vacation, it makes sense to be extra cautious.

For starters, no matter how desperate you are for a bit of excitement, you've got to be smart and realistic when you're deciding whether to go or not. If you know the person who has invited you, or they're a friend of a friend, or someone you know through your parents or relatives, then there's no good reason why you shouldn't go. But if you know very little about the person who has invited you—let's say you just met on the beach or something—it makes sense to give the whole thing a little more thought, and if you're away with your parents, talk it through with them. It's always a good idea to go with someone else—not just for safety, but because it's nice to have someone to stick with when you don't know many other people. And if you feel at all uneasy about it, don't go at all.

You should definitely travel by car as you probably won't be familiar with public transportation routes and schedules and won't have a clue which areas are safe or dangerous to walk in at night.

If your parents or someone else you're with has a rental car you should arrange for them to drop you off *and* pick you up afterward at an agreed time. If not, ask someone who knows the area to call you a taxi from a reputable firm, and ask the driver to pick you up at an agreed time—and make sure that all the details are clear before you get into the taxi, especially if there's a language problem. Take plenty of money out with you, and a taxi company's number and the number of the place you're staying (even if you think you'll be able to remember it by heart, you never know).

If you want to come home early, or you find yourself stranded after the party for any reason, *never* go wandering around outside alone—or even with a friend. And never, ever be tempted to hitchhike or accept a lift from someone you don't know. Instead, you should always call whoever is picking you up (or a taxi company) and wait indoors for your ride to arrive.

Chapter 2 Dating

Generally, the worst personal damage anyone ever suffers in the entire course of their dating career is a broken heart or two. But it must be said that there are other risks involved. It makes sense to know and think about those risks, so that you can avoid them, sit back, and enjoy the roller coaster thrills of your love life with no worries.

GETTING GEARED UP FOR A DATE

Making travel arrangements

"My mom told me that when she was young, boys always came and picked you up before a date and then took you home afterward. Even if they didn't have a car, they would come to your house anyway, just so you didn't have to travel on your own. She couldn't believe that boys don't normally do that any more, especially now that it's more dangerous for a girl to get around on her own in the dark. But then, it can be dangerous for boys too."

Anna, 14

"He lived in my apartment building, so we'd always taken the bus home together after we'd been out. Then one night—it was our fourth date, I think—he said he was staying at his dad's for the weekend, which meant that he had to take a different bus. Our building is miles

away from the bus stop and you have to walk past all these creepy alleys, so it's really dangerous if you're on your own. I was okay, thank God, but after that, I always asked him before we went out whether he was coming back to his mom's or not, so that I could get a ride home instead if he wasn't."

Cass, 15

No matter what else is on your mind before a date—and let's face it, there's probably going to be plenty—it's essential to give a bit of thought to how you are going to travel safely there and back.

Planning the outward leg of your journey shouldn't be too much hassle—arrange to meet at a familiar, easy-to-reach spot and follow all the usual safety precautions on your travels (see Chapters Three and Four for the lowdown on getting around).

Planning how you're going to get home can be more difficult. Whereas it used to be traditional for boys to walk girls home after a date, it's not really fair for girls to expect that now—after all, the streets can be dangerous for boys alone too.

As I said in the last chapter, the safest way to travel around in the evening alone is by car, so if your parents drive and are prepared to pick you up, it makes a lot of sense to take them up on their offer. However, even this can be tricky to arrange if you don't know exactly when you'll need to be picked up: you might not know beforehand where you're going on the date, or what time exactly you'll finish. And of course, there's all that embarrassment stuff, but in this case it makes a lot of sense to be very mature about it and put your safety first. If you're getting home any other way, check out

Chapter Four for transportation hints.

Deciding what to wear

"When I dress up to look good, I'm doing it for me. It makes me sick when boys think that girls dress up just to please them."

Polly, 16

We talked a bit about clothes in the last chapter, so flip back now if you skipped it! Although there shouldn't be any reason to be extra careful about what you wear to go on a date, it's probably wise to avoid ultrasexy gear unless you're going out with someone you know very well, consider an all-around nice guy, and feel you can really trust.

You should be aware of the sad fact that some boys are stuck in the dark ages, and still think that if a girl dresses sexily, she must be "easy" or "asking for it." Of course, it's just their tough luck if they're disappointed to find out that you're not, but it's no fun at all if you have to go through any nastiness because of it.

Most males have the morals and will power to keep their hormones under control, and will cheerfully let you go home without so much as a kiss, even if you've turned up on a date in the sexiest getup imaginable. But it's worth remembering that there are some guys out there who just don't have the intelligence or maturity. This could mean that you end up stuck with a date who gets sulky and nasty or disgustingly drooly and demanding. Or worse, it could mean facing a guy who won't take no for an answer: who will threaten, grab, or—worst-case scenario—rape you. Let's get something clear, though: raging hormones are no excuse for violating another person's rights, and if any of these vile things did happen to you, you would not be to blame, no matter what you were wearing.

BLIND DATES

"My friend set me up with her cousin, who was down from Canada for the holidays. He was good looking, but he was really creepy—he kept talking about all the girls he'd gone out with and things he'd done with them and asking me really personal questions, like if I was a virgin. And he was all over me. Luckily we were in McDonalds. If we'd gone somewhere quiet, I'd have been really scared. I nearly killed my friend after that!"

Jenny, 17

A blind date is nerve-racking enough to begin with, before you even start thinking about safety.

The best kind is the kind where you and your blind date make up a foursome with two people you know. This is far safer than going it alone, in every way. It means that you're not stuck in a situation where you have to chat with someone you might not get along with, so it's not as awkward, and it also means you're avoiding all sorts of potential dangers. You don't have to be a genius to figure out that meeting a virtual stranger in the evening, all on your own, has some risks. If you are going on a one-on-one blind date, always follow these rules:

• Like any other date, you should plan how you are going to get home. Unlike other dates though, you should sort out an arrangement that doesn't let your date get involved—in other words ask someone to pick you up, or plan to call a taxi or meet a friend who is also out and can travel home with you. This makes sense not only from a safety point of view (you don't get stuck alone with your date) but also because if you're not so keen on your date, you'll want to get away as swiftly as possible rather than have to put up with them walking or traveling with you.

• Choose somewhere busy to meet—it would be crazy to go somewhere quiet or secluded.

• Arrange to meet in a place you are familiar with, ideally somewhere where people know you.

• Always tell your family and friends exactly where you are going, and with whom.

• There's no point in being careful where you meet if you're going to end up alone with your date later. Even if you're getting along great, it's not a good idea to go back to your date's home, go for a walk in a deserted area, or get into his car (if he has one)—you still don't know enough about him to judge whether he's trustworthy.

• If you feel uneasy during the date—let's say the guy seems a bit creepy or you just get a funny feeling in your gut—don't ignore your instincts.

First, if you're not somewhere busy enough already, steer your date somewhere busier (as long as you don't need to walk through a quiet area to get there).

Next, make sure that your date is aware that other people know where you are (if someone is picking you up later, make sure your date knows that).

Otherwise you could say: "Oh, I hope you don't mind, but my friend might drop by later for a minute because she needed to give me something, and she said she might be passing." Finally, if your getting-home arrangements don't involve a ride or a taxi, get to a phone pronto and make sure that they do, or call a friend and ask him or her to turn up "by accident" just in time for you to travel home together.

The blind date safety rules aren't just for blind dates, by the way. You should also follow them if you've arranged a one-on-one date with someone you don't know very well, don't know much about, and didn't meet through your friends or family or through school or an organized after-school activity (sports, music lessons, a drama group, etc).

WHAT IS EXPECTED OF YOU ON A DATE?

"This boy took my sister out and paid for everything, but she didn't want to make out with him afterward and he got really moody, so in the end she did. Then we were watching Indecent Proposal *on video, where the billionaire offers Demi Moore a million dollars, and my sister said: 'He should have asked me—it would only have cost him the price of a movie ticket and a pizza.' I thought it was funny, but also really sad, when she put it like that."*

Harriet, 16

You probably wouldn't go on a date with someone you didn't like at least a little bit. But at first, the whole point of dating someone is to get to know that person a little bit better so that you can make your mind up for sure. It's quite possible to like someone a lot, even when you've barely spoken to them (you might even have met them at a party and ended up making out with them), and then go off them pretty quickly once you've had a chance to chat and find out what they're really like. Even if someone is perfectly nice, you can be put off by all sorts of things—a sense of humor you don't get (or no sense of humor at all), a lack of brain (or even being too brainy), an obsession with some hobby you find really dull, strong opinions that go against what you believe in, or just an outlook on life that is different from yours. The reason I'm saying all this is because it's easy to forget that going on a date isn't necessarily something you do because you want to have a kiss and cuddle at the end of it. Even when you've been seeing someone for a while, like them a lot, and thoroughly enjoy their company, it still doesn't necessarily mean that you'll want to get intimate with them.

So the answer to the question at the top of this section is: nothing. That doesn't mean that your date is expecting nothing—indeed, he might well be expecting all sorts of things. It just means that you shouldn't feel under pressure to do anything you don't want to do. Agreeing to go on a date doesn't mean you are agreeing to get intimate. Even if your date has paid for you to do something nice and eat yourself silly, it still stands—after all, you're not for sale at any price.

SAYING NO

"I've been really lucky, because none of the boys I've been out with have ever wanted to go any further with me than I wanted to go. But if they did, I wouldn't worry about telling them, and if they weren't prepared to wait until I knew them better and felt all right about it, I'd know that they weren't for me."

Dawn, 15

"Saying no is really important. I don't just mean about sex, I mean touching and all that as well. I was talking to my brother about it and he said that some girls say no when they mean yes. We had a massive fight, because I believe that no means no. If there really are girls who say no when they don't mean it, they are putting all other girls in danger because they give boys the wrong idea. I hope they feel guilty. They should."

Phoebe, 16

Here's another very important fact to remember: kissing someone doesn't mean you have to let them touch you, and letting someone touch you intimately doesn't mean that you have to go any further. As I said in the last chapter, you have a right to draw the line at any stage of intimacy, because it's your body. Anyone who crosses the line you have made is violating your rights.

Saying no to kissing

Let's start with kissing because it's a slightly different deal from the rest. Before someone kisses you, they probably have no idea at all whether you're interested in getting smoochy with them, unless they're psychic.

Most guys, when they lunge forward, lips open, are not *determined* to make out with you, no matter what. They're just trying to find out whether you want to kiss them, and, let's face it, asking outright would be even more embarrassing. You can give a clear answer by just moving your head away. It's like a conversation without words—him saying, "Do you want to kiss?" and you saying, "No thanks!"

If you've ever been on a date with someone you were desperate to kiss, but didn't know if they wanted to kiss you, then you'll know how tricky a situation it can be, and how hard it is to fathom. If you've ever made the first move (and I hope you have—this is the 90s after all! What are you waiting for?) then you'll know how much guts it takes and you'll know every last painful detail of the awkwardness, suspense, and jitters. If you don't know these feelings firsthand, try to imagine them and always be sympathetic to a guy who tries to kiss you on a date, even when you don't want to kiss him. Just see it for what it is: a question he's asking you in body language.

Saying no to going further

Silent conversations have gone on between couples since time began, and will probably continue to go on into eternity. Nobody talks about it, but everybody knows the rules. The same goes for taking things further *during* necking. It was probably a feisty cavegirl babe who first grabbed her date's wandering hand and stopped it in its tracks as it inched its way across her tiger-fur blouse thing. And the rest of the species has been instinctively doing it ever since.

Just because you're not talking with words, it doesn't

mean that you're not making yourself clear. If a guy chooses to ignore your body language it's as outrageously rude as if he'd ignored a request you'd made out loud. When someone keeps on trying to kiss you or feel you up when you plainly don't want him to, you have every right to start getting huffy.

First, make your body language even clearer (push him away from you). If that doesn't work, use your voice. Say "No," or "Please..." or "Don't do that!" or "Get off!" or whatever else comes into your head—just make it clear, because he's obviously either very stupid or he's getting ridiculously carried away and needs to be dragged back to reality, quickly.

If someone ignores all your protestations, your internal alarm bells should be going off: Here is a guy who isn't taking no for an answer. Get annoyed, stand up, and get out of the situation as quickly as possible. Worried about what he'll think of you? Forget it. He's not worth it.

DATE RAPE

"A girl at the local college was raped by a boy she went out with and it was in the papers. One of my friends said that it can't have been as bad as being raped by someone you've never met. I couldn't believe she said that—I'd hate to be raped by anybody, and I thought that the girl must have been so scared and upset, getting attacked by someone she thought she could trust. In that way, it's maybe even a bit worse. I hope the guy gets put away for years—he deserves it."

Tanya, 17

"When I was younger, I went on a date with a guy eight years older than me. I did like him, but I was a virgin and I didn't want to sleep with him—I actually didn't plan to sleep with anybody until I was in a proper relationship. After we'd been to the movies he asked me back to his apartment. Perhaps it was stupid of me to go, I don't know.

Anyway, when we got there, things started getting heavy, which was nice, until he tried to take my clothes off. I didn't want him to, and he went nuts, shouting at me that I must have known what he had asked me back for, and why did I come if I didn't want to have sex. I was incredibly upset and confused, and he kept saying: 'I know you want to really...' and just forced himself on me. It was so horrible. I kept protesting the whole time, but I didn't fight because I was frightened and he was much bigger than me. Anyway, I couldn't really believe what was happening, I kept thinking, 'This can't really be happening to me,' and it was almost like I was somewhere else.

I didn't tell anyone about it and it actually took me several years before I even admitted to myself that I'd been raped. Before that, I kept thinking, 'Well, maybe I did know what I was letting myself in for, going back there,' and blaming myself for not fighting back. Now I have come to terms with the fact that I was not to blame, and I am angry as hell about it."

Kim, 21

Date rape is a term that was invented fairly recently to describe rapes or sexual assaults in which the attacker is someone the victim knows and has been out with. It's a word that many people don't like because by giving this kind of attack a special name, it almost infers that it's different (and therefore maybe less serious) than straightforward rape, when in fact, *any* rape is hateful, wrong, and very serious indeed.

Date rape is often a result of a guy refusing to take no for an answer. Even if a girl has willingly gotten into an intimate situation, she still has the right to say no—and if her partner doesn't respect that right and forces her into having sex, it is rape. That fact remains true whether the rapist uses physical force, violence, a weapon, or threats to get what he wants, or if he uses emotional manipulation—making his victim feel guilty or confused.

Protecting yourself

It's depressing to think that you can take all the care in the world not to walk in deserted areas at night, etc. and then end up getting raped by someone you know in a place where you should be safe. Still, there *are* some precautions you can take:

• Don't get into situations where you're all alone with a date you don't know very well, or don't entirely trust. This includes getting into his car, going to his home, letting him into your home when there's no one else there, and going into a bedroom at a party.

• If you've said no to something intimate, never go back on your word. Make it clear that you are not prepared to be persuaded to do things that you don't want to do.

• If a date pushes you to go further than you want to, even when you've made your feelings clear, take it as a warning sign. Avoid being alone with him again, and think seriously about whether you might be better off ditching him and finding someone more understanding.

Preparing for the Worst

If you are attacked by someone you know, it can be so shocking that the reality of the situation doesn't sink in right away. It's important, however, to try and gather your thoughts so that you can try to stop the attack from going any further. You'll find everything you need to know about this, and about what to do if you are raped or assaulted, in Chapter Seven.

Chapter

Out and About 3

BE PREPARED

Being careful when you're out and about is obviously important. But many people don't realize that some of the most crucial steps toward personal safety need to be taken before you even leave your home.

The Three-Point Safety Plan

Before you go out, even if you're in a hurry, you should *always*:

• Know exactly where you're going and how you're getting there. If you're headed for an area you don't know well, make some phone calls or look at a map—don't just leave it until you get there.

• Know exactly how you're going to get back.

• Let someone else—preferably a member of your family—know exactly where you're going, what you're doing, and how you're getting there and back. If there's no one around to tell, leave a note, or a message on an answering machine—it's a good idea to have an answering machine at home, for this very reason. If your plans change while you're out, don't forget to give your family an update on your movements.

Getting kitted out

Another important way to be prepared is to make sure you're carrying everything you might need. The essential kit includes:

• Your housekeys. And while we're on the subject of keys, it's worth getting one of those key rings that has a little built-in flashlight or spotlight—they're handy for seeing the keyhole properly in the dark, which means you can get indoors nice and quickly without fumbling around for ages.

• Money. And of course, a cash machine card or checkbook, if you have one.

• A travel pass, if you have one. Otherwise, it's a good idea to carry a bit of cash separate from your main money, which you keep reserved for emergencies—just in case you unexpectedly needed extra cash for a bus or train fare (or maybe a taxi) after you'd spent the cash you had on you.

• Enough change for a phone call or two—again keep this separate from your main stash. It's also smart to have a calling card for public phones. Most telephone companies offer a calling card with your phone service. Ask your parents if they can give you a card to carry with you or if they will just let you have their PIN (personal identification number). This is your home phone number plus four digits. The card and PIN allow you to charge calls from a pay phone or a regular phone to your parents' phone number. But don't go overboard on the charging or your parents might be a bit ticked. When you are dialing using the calling card, be careful of people standing behind you who might be trying to watch the numbers you dial or listen to the number you give to the operator. Stand directly in front of the phone. Your parents might wind up getting charged for calls you never made if someone gets a hold of the number. If this were to happen, have them call the phone company right away. You might have to get your number changed.

• A personal alarm, if you have one—see Chapter Eight for more details.

Obviously, it makes sense to keep all this important stuff as safe as possible. If you carry a bag, use one that goes over your shoulder, and wear it across your body—that way it's harder for someone to grab it. Better still, wear a fanny pack or backpack. If you have an inside pocket, keep your purse or wallet in there instead of in your bag or in an outside pocket. Otherwise, it's worth using a safety pin to secure it inside your pocket. It's also wise to keep your keys, travel pass, and phone card in a safe pocket, just in case your bag got lost or stolen.

If you're lucky enough to have an especially nice watch, or flashy jewelry, it's sensible to keep it hidden when you're walking around. If your clothes don't do the job, you can always turn a watch or ring upside down, so that it's not so visible.

WHEN YOU'RE OUT

Once you're past your front door and you're out in the great wide world, it can be easy to get so wrapped up in what you're doing that you forget to think about safety.

But once you know the basics, it doesn't take long for them to become second nature—so you can get on with enjoying yourself.

Getting around on foot

When you're out walking, you should always be alert, thinking ahead, and taking notice of what's going on around you. But let's not beat around the bush: If you want to stay safe, there are some situations where you've always got to be *extra* alert. They are:

• Being out alone in the dark, especially in quiet areas and poorly lit streets.

• Being alone in an area you're not all that familiar with—especially on vacation, when you may have no idea of what the area is like.

• Walking past alleys, empty building sites, dark, deep doorways, and anywhere else that a person could lurk without being seen.

And, even in daylight, there's one thing you should always avoid doing, and that's taking risky shortcuts. It's always smarter to go the long way from a to b (even if it means getting to where you're going a little late or feeling a little more tired) if the only alternative is a shortcut which involves:

• Big open spaces (like parks and fields).

• An alleyway—especially a quiet one.

- An empty building site.

- An underground pass.

- A roadway that people don't use much on foot (like a busy highway) where a car could pull over next to you.

- An elevated bridge over a busy road where people can't see you clearly from the street.

- An unlit street at night.

And whenever you're walking, you should always follow these guidelines:

- Know your way. If you're not familiar with the area, take a good look at a map beforehand.

- Keep your mind on your surroundings—look and listen to what's going on around you and take it all in. Daydreaming and wearing a Walkman can make this impossible, so unless you're walking in a very busy area, it's best to give them a rest. The same goes for browsing through a magazine or book while you're walking, of course—and it also comes with the added hazard of walking into a lamppost. (Not actually life-threatening, I know, but it could cost you several thousand coolness points.)

- Especially at night, take an extra good look around as you go along, trying to spot places or groups of people you could make a beeline for if you suddenly felt nervous or threatened.

• Be extra alert when you're turning off a main street into a quieter side street, paying special attention to people behind you. If you've been feeling suspicious about someone, it's often better to stop and let them pass you before you make the turn.

• Walk facing oncoming traffic—that way, people in cars can see you (and could help if you were in trouble). It also means that if a car pulled up alongside you, you'd have seen it coming, and would have far more time to think straight than if it had come up behind you. (For the lowdown on what to do if a car pulls over next to you, see *Threatening situations*, on page 47).

• When the streets are quiet, and especially when it's dark, always walk in the center of the pavement. This means you avoid getting too near parked cars on the road side of the pavement, and doorways and alleys—all places where it would be possible for someone lurking to pull you in.

Getting money from cash machines

There's no doubt that cash machines are a darn handy invention. But remember that when you're getting cash out of a hole in the wall, you might as well be wearing a sign that says: "Hello! I've got some money on me!" In other words, you could attract nasty folks who are after cash and prepared to rob you for it. So always:

• Avoid using automated teller machines (ATMs) after dark, unless you absolutely have to.

- Try to use ATMs that are in safe locations: busy streets (not side streets) or better still, inside the bank itself.

- Have your cash card in your hand, ready to use, so that you don't need to spend loads of unnecessary time fumbling around.

- Look around you when you're withdrawing cash to make sure that there's no one about who is taking just a bit too much interest in what you're doing. Once you've punched in your details, turn your back to the cash machine so you've got an even better view of what's going on behind you.

- Put your money straight into your wallet, bag, or pocket. Never stand around counting it—cash machines rarely make mistakes anyway, so it's certainly not worth the risk.

THREATENING SITUATIONS

With any luck (and a bit of caution) there's no reason why you should ever have a brush with a nasty situation. But it makes sense to know what to do.

Getting whistles, leers, and catcalls

Unfortunately, the world is full of people who feel that it's okay to express their feelings out loud to strangers they find attractive. Some of them do it because they're basically not bright enough to realize that no one wants to know what they think, that people have the right to walk down the street without being hassled, and that their comments could be threatening or offensive. Others realize all that, but just don't care.

In other words, people who leer, whistle, or make suggestive comments usually don't mean any harm, and many girls and women take it as a compliment—albeit a compliment from a bit of a jerk. Having said that, there's no denying that it can sometimes feel threatening or scary when you're the target, especially if you're alone, or you're faced by a big, noisy group of leerers, or the things being said are pretty offensive.

However you feel, the best thing to do is just ignore the comments and keep on walking. Shouting something back or giving dirty looks will only invite more comments—possibly less complimentary ones.

Getting an insulting comment yelled at you

For the same reasons that people whistle and make lewd remarks, others think nothing of insulting strangers on the street—about the way they look, or maybe about their race or color. Because these comments are meant to hurt, they are always pretty scary. After all, it makes you wonder how much it would take for the shouter to cross the line between *saying* stuff and actually getting physical. It's upsetting, too—even if you know that they're talking nonsense, it hurts to think that there's someone out there, someone who doesn't even know you, who apparently doesn't like you.

Nasty comments should always be ignored; first, because by ignoring the idiot who made the comment, you're keeping your dignity and showing that you really don't care what they think of you; and second, because if you give any kind of reply—but particularly a belligerent one—it could look like an invitation to start an argument or fight, which would be bad news.

Being faced with an aggressive person

Every year thousands of people, generally guys, get hurt in incidents which start quite innocently—a fight over someone cutting in line or bumping into someone else, a person getting dragged into someone else's argument, a person trying to help a drunk, upset, or angry person. If you know exactly what to do in the event that you're faced with someone aggressive, it's often possible to diffuse the situation and avoid getting hurt. Knowing that you're clued in on the right thing to do in these cases can make you feel a lot more self-assured. Here are some pointers that are definitely worth filing in your brain, just in case:

• If you can possibly walk away safely from the situation early on, do. You may feel annoyed and want to sort things out, but the feeling of frustration will pass. It's far better than risking getting hurt. Important: whenever you are walking away from an aggressive person, walk backward until you're at a safe distance away from them or behind a closed door. It may sound silly, but it makes sense—if you turn your back, they'll have a better chance to charge at you and hurt you, if the urge takes them, and you won't know about it until it's way too late.

• If you can't walk away, be on your guard from the start—you never know what an aggressive person who is wound up might do next.

• Try to keep a safe distance from the person, while staying near enough to talk to him.

• Never touch a person who is angry or upset. Even a light pat on the shoulder that you meant to be reassuring could be enough to make him blow up into violence.

• Never act combative back—two aggressive people is the recipe for a fight, and your number one goal is to avoid getting hurt. Instead, talk slowly, softly, and clearly, staying as cool as you can, and be cautious about what you say.

• Watch your body language—if you cross your arms, plant your hands on your hips or wag your finger at someone, it sends out aggressive signals that are just as strong as if you'd said them out loud.

• Keep your cool even if the aggressor is deliberately trying to wind you up.

• It pays to think ahead about the possibility that the aggressor might get violent. Look around you: If there is something nearby that the person could use as a weapon, it's important that you try and move the argument elsewhere. But remember, as before: don't turn your back when you're moving. Walk slowly backward, instead. Look around for possible escape routes, too, and decide which way you'd run.

• If things do turn violent, as with any attack, your aim is to get away as fast as you can.

A stranger tries to talk to you

It's never a great idea to stop and talk to a stranger, although obviously you should use your common sense—for instance, a woman laden down with shopping bags and babies, asking for directions, is unlikely to be a potential attacker. But it pays to be cautious. It's always smart to be suspicious of males who ask you for the time or for directions—of course, they may be genuine, but who wants to take risks? Keep walking briskly while you tell them that you're sorry but you don't have a watch/don't know.

The same goes for males who try to start a conversation—move on, yelling over your shoulder that you're sorry but you're in a big hurry. Be extra alert when it comes to ruses like: "Don't I know you from somewhere?" "Wait, I think you dropped something!" and flattery or chattiness. Even if the guy is young, seems nice, and looks pretty fit, use your head: The street is *not* a great place to meet guys! Be doubly cautious of groups of guys, and finally, watch out for friendly-seeming males who warn you about the dangers of walking alone and offer to keep you company—this is a nasty, popular trick with attackers.

A car pulls up alongside you

There are no two ways about it: You should never stop for, or approach, a car that pulls up next to you. In fact, your prime objective should be to get as far away from it as possible, pronto, and keep walking. Think about it: It wouldn't be hard for the driver to fling his door open and pull you in, if he wanted to. Of course, the driver might just be innocently pulling up to ask for directions, but that's his tough luck—he'll just have to ask someone else.

If a car crawls along next to you after you've ignored it, go into the nearest shop and wait until it's gone, or turn around and start walking in the other direction (remember that it'll take a car much longer to do the same, and it may not be possible at all).

And, of course, it should go without saying that you should never accept a ride from a stranger (see Chapter Four for more on rides).

You think you're being followed

Being followed is one of the most terrifying experiences you can imagine. If you start to suspect that it's happening to you, it's always better to trust your instincts than tell yourself not to be silly and paranoid. Sure, you may be wrong, but if you were right, it would be crazy to take the risk of going merrily on your way, talking yourself out of it, wouldn't it?

As soon as you get the first hint of a suspicion that you're being followed, speed up your pace a little by taking bigger strides (don't break into a trot or a run just yet) and cross the street, looking as confident and purposeful as you can. If you walk diagonally, you'll be able to see whether the person behind you is thinking of crossing too, without giving away that you're feeling vulnerable by looking over your shoulder.

If someone crosses the street after you do, you should take it as a fairly certain sign that you're being followed. Don't be afraid to let those internal alarm bells of yours go off, but don't panic. Instead, spring into straight-thinking, all-stations-set-for-action mode:

• Speed up your walking pace some more.

• If you carry a personal alarm (see Chapter Eight), get it out while you're walking and hold it in your hand, ready to use (but don't slow down while you're searching for it).

• If you're wearing a Walkman, take it off now—you're going to need all five senses, including your hearing!

• At the same time, start looking around for a group of people (ideally a group that includes women), a police officer, or a shop, restaurant, pub, hotel, or garage which is open and head over quickly. Once you've reached the people or premises, explain that you're being followed and ask for help.

• In the scary event that there's not a soul around and nowhere to go, keep walking briskly until you see a house with a light on. Walk confidently up to the front door, as if it were your house, and ring the bell. I know of one girl who did this, and to her horror, found that there was still no reply by the time the person following her caught up. In an inspired moment, however, she cleverly thought of shouting: "Tony! Jim! Steve! Dave! Alan! Dan! It's me! Open up! I'm being followed!" Obviously put off by the thought that there was a huge bunch of guys on the other side of the door, the creep slunk right past her and left her alone!

• While you're heading for safety, keep very aware of what the person behind you is doing. Listen carefully to his steps and check his reflection in the windows of parked cars and shops to see whether he is speeding up. This is better than looking back over your shoulder, which can throw you off balance and slow you down. Match his speed, but don't start to run unless he does—it'll use up your energy and give away that you're frightened and panicking.

• When and if a person following you breaks into a run, you should go into red alert mode:
- Run as fast as you can.
- If you're carrying heavy stuff which is slowing you down, chuck it—your safety is more important than what you're carrying, *whatever* it is.
- Shout loudly and wave your arms to attract attention.
- If you have a personal alarm, set it off.
- If you can't see any signs of safety up ahead, dart off the pavement and into the road and try to get the attention of people in cars. Obviously, though, stay near the curb and be careful not to get run over—getting squashed by a car isn't really a much better option than getting attacked!

ON YOUR DOORSTEP

It makes sense to be wise about safety from the minute you leave the house until the minute you get back, so don't skimp on taking precautions just because you've reached your front door:

• Have your key ready in your hand so that you can let yourself in nice and fast, without having to stand around fumbling in your bag or pockets for years.

• If you're carrying a lot of heavy stuff that might slow

you down in opening the door, put it down, unlock the door, and let yourself in first and bring your load in afterward.

• If you think that you may have been followed home, and there's no one home, pretend that there is: Make a big deal of shouting, "Hello! I'm back!" Or if the lights are off, you could shout: "Come on, wake up everyone!" If you're really worried, you should check whether a neighbor has the lights on and knock on that door instead.

Chapter

4 Getting from A to B—Transportation

USING PUBLIC TRANSPORTATION

By and large, public transportation is pretty safe, but it makes sense to be aware of potential dangers, and do everything you can to avoid them. These are the basic essential travel safety rules:

• It's always better to travel with someone else, if you can.

• It's a good idea to have a map and details of train and bus routes and schedules at home (you can pick these up from most stations). If you're traveling to somewhere you haven't been before, check out your route and which train or bus you need to take *before* you leave home. If you don't have a map, phone the station or local bus company and ask for information. If you don't plan ahead, and you end up having to stand around staring at a map, looking lost, it could be just the excuse an unsound person needs to start talking to you, pretending to offer help or asking where you're going.

If you plan to use local public transportation on vacation, don't even *think* of going out before you've armed yourself with maps and schedules, and, ideally, got the lowdown from someone who knows the system well and can give you advice, tips, and warnings.

• If you use public transportation a lot, it makes sense to have a travel pass. Otherwise, always try to have exact change for your fare with you. Have it ready so that you don't need to fumble around in your bag or wallet when you're buying a ticket.

• Always be alert and aware of what's going on around you. Remember that if you wear a Walkman and stare off into space, you're not going to be as alert as you could be!

• You should always walk—or run—away at the first sign of any trouble. It's never a good idea to get physical with someone unless you absolutely need to, in order to defend yourself.

Safety on trains

"The car was totally empty—it was just me and this man. And even though he seemed okay, he kept looking over at me, and I didn't feel all that comfortable. I kept telling myself that I was being paranoid, but in the end I was just so nervous that I got up and moved into the next car. A few stops later, this woman came running in, she was in a real panic, and said: 'There's a man in the next car who just exposed himself!' Now I always trust my feelings, because if I hadn't that time, it would probably have been me who got flashed at."

Kirstie, 17

The good news is that crime on the railways is a pretty rare thing—recent surveys and reports have proved that. The other bit of good news is that old, dark, scary-seeming trains and stations are all being revamped. They're sorting out all kinds of new security measures, from the simple (like extra lighting) to the high-tech (like security cameras linked to police departments). Nevertheless, it's still superimportant to be alert, aware, and careful—that way, you can be extra sure of being safe. So:

• If the station is quiet, try to sit near groups of people—preferably groups that include women. Or if there is a guard or another official person about, hang around close to them.

• Many stations have emergency phones that you can use to contact transit police or station staff. Don't be afraid to use them if you feel threatened or nervous. No one will hassle you for a false alarm.

• It's always worth taking that extra bit of time to check out all the train cars and pick the busiest one to sit in, especially at night. Of course, the busiest car can suddenly become the emptiest one if people all get off at once, so be prepared to change cars during your journey.

• There are still a few trains left running which have some compartments that don't have any doors to a corridor or another car. Eventually, these will be phased out but in the meantime, if you need to travel on one of these trains, be sure to avoid these isolated compartments. There will always be an open car you can sit in instead, so make sure you do.

• Always take a good look around at the other people in your car and trust your judgment and gut instinct if you think anyone seems unstable, drunk, drugged up, aggressive, or just a bit weird—particularly men. If you don't like the look of someone, change cars. It's also pretty wise to avoid sitting in a car with a group of young guys who are all together, especially if they seem rowdy. Of course, most of the time the people you think look iffy are probably 100 percent harmless—but who wants to take chances?

• If you can't find a car that you feel entirely safe about sitting in, choose the one nearest to the conductor.

• Always choose a seat that's near the door—so you can get off quickly if you need to—and if possible, one that's in easy reach of the emergency alarm, just in case.

• If you get any sense that you're in danger—say you switch cars a couple of times and someone follows you, or someone actually starts acting strange or threatening, change cars. If that's not possible, go and sit with the nearest and largest trustworthy-looking group of people. There's no need to feel embarrassed about doing this and you can always tell them why you want to sit with them—they're bound to be very understanding.

• If there is no one else around, or no one who looks like they'd be much help if someone attacked you, don't be afraid to use the emergency alarm. Many people are put off by the warning signs which say that there is a fine for improper use, but rest assured that once you explained that you were feeling threatened and scared and felt that you were in danger, you wouldn't even be told off—let alone fined.

• If you are actually attacked, you should scream for help as loudly as you can. If you are near the emergency alarm, and can get to it, you should obviously use it. If you can't, it's worth shouting: "Use the emergency alarm!" because someone who might be too scared to wade in and actually help you may not have thought about helping you in this way instead.

• If you're not in direct, immediate danger, it makes sense to wait until the train pulls into a station before you sound the emergency alarm, as help will be more easily available there.

• Where your safety is concerned, it's never worth taking chances. Just think about how you'd kick yourself if something nasty happened after you'd *thought* about changing cars, getting off the train, or using the alarm, but decided not to bother and just to hope for the best instead.

• If your local station is unmanned—that is, there are no permanent staff working there—and not usually very busy, it's always smart to arrange for someone to come and meet you. And ask them to be early—just in case you are.

Safety on buses

"Once when I was waiting for the bus, this guy stopped his car by the bus stop and asked if I wanted a lift. I just turned around and ran into the store and he drove off, but I felt so shaky. He must have known that no girl would take a ride from a stranger, so he must have had

something wrong with him. I still have these nightmares where he pulls me into the car. I get the jitters thinking that he's still out there, somewhere. I wonder if he's hurt anyone. I keep thinking I see his car, too, following me, but it never is him. I think I just imagine it."

Sue, 16

"I was sitting at the back of the bus by myself and this bunch of older boys got on. When I got up for my stop they all blocked my way. They were saying all these scary things, and I was really frightened. What I couldn't believe was that no one else on the bus did anything about it. In the end they did let me get past but now I always sit right by the doors."

Paul, 14

By and large, the bus is a safe way to travel, and safer still when you follow these guidelines:

• Anywhere that you're alone, particularly when it's dark, is potentially dangerous. If you need to wait at a quiet bus stop at night, it's a good idea to check if there is a store or cafe open where you'll be able to wait inside and see the bus coming. If not, be sure to stand facing oncoming cars so that you're lit by their headlights, and close to the road so that they can see you (but not too close, obviously—it would be a bummer to get run over in the name of protecting yourself!). Above all, be alert and keep your wits about you. In other words, don't get engrossed in a magazine, turn on your Walkman, or decide to catch forty winks on a comfortable bench: you might not notice if someone suspicious turns up, and you'd lose the vital chance to get away. You should also think about what you'd do if you were in danger, or if you were actually attacked—where would you run to? Is there a store, pub, garage, hotel, or restaurant open nearby? Make a note of the nearest one.

• If you're traveling alone it's a good idea to choose an aisle seat. On unpopular bus routes or night buses, where the bus can be pretty empty, always pick a seat close to the driver.

• If you feel that you're under threat, go and stand right next to the driver and tell him or her what's going on.

• Remember that buses occasionally have to terminate before their final stops—that means that everyone has to get off, and you may still be quite a way from where you're going. This doesn't happen often, but if you don't have a travel pass, it's a good idea always to carry enough cash for an extra fare, otherwise you could end up stranded.

• If you know that you're going to be getting off a bus alone at a quiet bus stop, always try to get someone to meet you there.

DEALING WITH UNSTABLE PEOPLE ON PUBLIC TRANSPORTATION

People who talk to you

Usually when people start chatting with you on public transportation, or when you're waiting at a station or bus stop, the worst thing that's going to happen is you'll get your bent ear chewed off and be bored stiff. Still, it's sometimes worth being a little bit suspicious. Remember:

• If you don't like the look of someone, or if someone makes you feel uneasy, don't let him start a proper conversation with you. First, try giving unresponsive one-word answers and being a bit standoffish. If he doesn't get the hint, whip out a book, magazine, or exercise book, if you have one, and tell him there's something you've got to read/write. Or put on your Walkman, if you have one. If you don't have anything suitable to get engrossed in, you could say that you're sorry, but you're trying to work something out, and then start making a big show of muttering to yourself and counting on your fingers. If he still refuses to leave you in peace, excuse yourself, get up, and stand by the door as if you're getting ready to get off at your stop.

• Never tell a stranger your name, address, school, or place of work, and be careful not to let a stranger overhear any of this stuff if you're telling someone else. You should also not let a stranger know or overhear if you regularly spend time alone at home (i.e., before your parents get home from work).

• If someone says something unpleasant, weird, or threatening to you, don't be afraid to get up right away and change seats. If he follows you, stand up again and announce loudly: "Go away!" or "I don't know this person, and he won't leave me alone!" and look around to other passengers for support.

People who touch you

"The bus was packed, everyone was standing, all squashed up, and I felt someone touch my butt. I couldn't even tell who it was, but I'm sure it was on purpose, because it was like they squeezed it—it wasn't like someone just brushing past by accident. It really made me feel sick, and when I got home, I couldn't wait to take a bath. I felt sort of dirty, and I wanted to cry. Until it happens to you, you wouldn't think it would be such a big deal."

Suzanne, 15

"I was standing up on the train when this hand just came out of nowhere and grabbed my boob! I'm usually not all that brave, but I was so shocked and annoyed that I just grabbed the hand and turned around and said 'What are you doing???' It turned out to be this woman who was trying to grab the pole next to me, and she'd tripped or something! We were both really embarrassed, but she said: 'Don't worry dear, you did the right thing. There are some funny people around.' She made me feel much better. At least if it had been some perv, he wouldn't have gotten away with it. I'd definitely do the same if it happened again."

Amy, 18

Among the not very lovely array of people on this planet who get off on doing unsociable things to others, there is a particular breed called the *frotteur*. A *frotteur* is someone who likes to touch strangers, or rub up against them, and crowded places are the easiest for them to get an opportunity to do their stuff. Because of this, they often turn up on busy trains or buses. Although they are rarely dangerous, being the victim of a *frotteur* is still a very, very unpleasant experience. Here's how to avoid them:

- It's sometimes hard to tell whether someone has touched you on purpose or by accident (because everyone is packed together and the train or bus is wobbling around all over the place). Even if you're not sure, it makes sense to move away, if you can. If it *was* some creep touching you deliberately, why stick around long enough for him to do it again?

- If someone is definitely touching you, groping you, or rubbing up against you, move away immediately.

- If you can't move away, the best way to make him stop is to embarrass him. Look the offender in the eye, if you can, and yell: "Stop that!" or "Get away from me!"

- It's actually a good idea to embarrass a *frotteur* even if you *can* move away because you're doing other people a service too—an embarrassed *frotteur* who has been found out will probably get off the bus or train, or if he stays on, will be avoided by other people. If you just quietly move away, he's bound to turn his attentions to some other poor soul. So swallow your pride and do *everyone* a favor by speaking out.

TAXIS

"There's always a big row of gypsy cabs outside the disco, but you'd never catch me getting in one. I mean, anyone

could pretend to be a cab driver, couldn't he? You'd have to be crazy to get into a car with a guy you didn't know."

Faye, 17

Licensed taxis are a great, safe way to travel, and a better bet at night than public transportation, if you can afford it. Still, it's always better to share a cab with a friend—it's safer and, of course, it's cheaper, too. Here are some other important cab safety facts:

• You should never pick up a taxi on the street unless it's a proper, licensed cab that has a special identity number displayed on the inside and outside.

• Gypsy cabs may or may not be licensed, which means that the people who drive them have all been checked out. Regarding those that are not licensed, anyone can become a driver without having a background check. Of course, most gypsy cab drivers are perfectly decent folks, but it obviously makes sense to be a bit more wary. Always use a reputable cab company—one that is well-known or has been recommended to you by someone.

• On vacation, you should always ask a local person or someone who works at your hotel or apartment complex for advice about taxis before you even think of taking one alone. Ask whether or not they are licensed, and try to get a personal recommendation of a reputable firm.

• It's a good idea to learn the number of a reputable cab firm by heart, or keep a note of the number with you. Choose one that has long operating hours, just in case you ever need a cab in the middle of the night.

Even if you live in a city where it's possible to hail licensed cabs, it's a better idea to order a taxi by phone than to stand around alone at night in the hopes of hailing one.

• When you're phoning for a cab from a public place, you should always take care to talk quietly to avoid anyone overhearing your call. Remember that anyone could turn up and pretend to be your cab. For the same reason, always ask the cab company to tell you the name of your driver and what make and color of car he'll be in. That way, you'll be able to check for sure that the driver who shows up is the genuine article.

• Never accept a ride from someone who approaches you on the street or drives up alongside you and asks you if you need a taxi. Even if they say they work for a gypsy cab firm, there's no way of telling, is there? (Don't be taken in by the sight of a radio handset in the vehicle—anyone could get hold of a fake one and put it in their car). At best, the driver could be unlicensed and uninsured. At worst, well, think about it: What easier way could there be for a weirdo to get someone into a car?

• If you ever get into an unlicensed cab by mistake be wary, wily, and totally alert. The same goes for traveling in any cab that doesn't come from a company you know and trust, or if you just get a funny feeling about a driver. See the section called *Supercautious passenger safety hints*, further on.

• Once you've arrived home, ask the cab driver to hang around until he can see that you're safely inside—it makes good sense, and you can bet that the driver won't mind at all.

HITCHHIKING

"My cousin was going backpacking around Europe on her own, and she said that if she had to hitchhike, she'd only go in cars being driven by women, or a man and a lady. It didn't do her much good, though—one woman was drunk and nearly had a car crash, and she also got a lift from a bunch of people in a minivan, and the man driving tried to feel her up, even though there were other girls in there. She said she definitely wouldn't do it again, because you can never tell what people are going to be like."

Chloe, 15

Hitchhiking is a really, really bad idea. It's just not worth risking your safety for the sake of a free ride. It's slightly less risky for guys or a group of people, but it's still not at all advisable. After all, you just don't know whose car you're getting into.

Accepting rides from friendly-seeming strangers is the same story. It can be ever so tempting, especially when you're late, or it's pouring rain and freezing cold, and your bus hasn't turned up. But I know I'd rather be cold, wet, and late than dead or in a hospital. Who wouldn't?

If you do hitch, or accept a ride from a stranger (and I hope to god that you wouldn't be that crazy)—always follow the *Supercautious passenger safety hints* below.

Supercautious passenger safety hints

- Before you get into the car, make a mental note of

the license plate number and the make and model of the car—just in case you need it.

- Always sit in the back, rather than the front passenger seat. The only exception would be if the car is a two-door model, in which case you should sit in the front so that the driver couldn't lock the doors and prevent you from getting out. If you feel funny about telling a driver where you want to sit, saying you suffer from car sickness if you sit in the back/front is always a good excuse.

- Take note of where the lock and door handle is on your door, in case you need to use them in a hurry.

- Open the window as soon as you get in, in case you need to attract attention (again, just say that you get carsick if you don't have it open).

- If you chat with the driver, don't mention any personal details about yourself—where you live, where you go to school, etc.

- If the driver starts to act a bit odd—saying strange things, staring at you, brushing against you when changing gear, driving in totally the wrong direction for where you're going, or driving badly—and you feel uneasy, don't ignore it and hope for the best. Wait until you reach a busy, familiar place and say firmly that you've decided you'd like to get out there instead. If the streets are empty, or you don't know where you are, wait until you can see a pub, store, restaurant, hotel, or garage that's open up ahead and ask to get out there.

If you feel odd about doing it for no apparent reason, you could always tell the driver that your brother works there and it's just occurred to you that you can get a lift home with him instead. Once you're out, phone a cab or your parents.

- If you get a real danger alert signal, something that really sets off alarm bells in your head (i.e., the driver refuses to let you out in the above circumstances, makes a frightening or lewd remark or ignores you if you tell him that he's going the wrong way) try to stay calm and think on your feet. Open the window and wave and shout wildly to try and let other drivers know you're in trouble. If you have no luck getting anyone's attention and help, you should think about trying to get out—although never while the car is moving. Instead, every time the car stops for traffic lights or to give way, look around quickly to see if there is anything open or a group of people, or a police officer. If there is, whip the door open and run out toward the safe spot. Once you've calmed down, call a cab or your parents.

RIDES

"I went to my girlfriend's last Christmas, and I had to be back for Christmas dinner with my mom and dad. My girlfriend's uncle offered to drive me home, but he'd been drinking since first thing in the morning. I didn't want to walk in the cold, so it was tempting, but in the end I turned him down, because a boy at my school was killed by a drunk driver, and I didn't want it to be my fault, someone taking their car out when they were plastered."

Matthew, 16

"He was one of the builders who had built the new gym at school last year. They were all really funny and friendly. It was pouring rain and he stopped his van and shouted 'need a lift, sweetie?' I felt like I knew him well enough, so it wasn't like taking a ride from a stranger—I'd never do that. Anyway, big mistake—he started asking about if I had a boyfriend and touching my leg. That was all, but it was horrible. I shook like a leaf."

Anita, 14

There are very few people dumb enough to climb merrily into a stranger's car, but lots of perfectly bright people have found themselves in nasty situations when they accept a ride from someone they know a little bit. The ground rule here is that, unless you know someone pretty well, it's not too smart to get into a car with them. If you're not sure about someone, and you still choose to get into the car, always follow the *Supercautious passenger safety hints* above.

The other very important thing to remember when it comes to accepting lifts is never to get into a car when you suspect that the driver might be drunk. If you know for sure that someone's been drinking, you definitely shouldn't accept the ride. Of course, this can be a tricky situation. Maybe you've got no other way of getting home, or let's say you've been baby-sitting—wouldn't it be rude (and maybe jeopardize your job) to tell your employer: "I'm sorry but I'd rather you didn't drive me home, because you might be acting normal but you stink of booze/you missed putting the key in the car door by about three feet/if I'm not very much mistaken you're obviously completely and utterly blotto."

The bottom line is, once again, that your safety is the most important thing. Can you see yourself sitting up in your hospital bed saying, "Oh well, I've had seventy stitches in my face and I think we killed that family of five in the other car, but at least I didn't offend anyone. Thank heavens for that!" I don't think so.

If you're really worried about appearing rude, make sure you don't wait until you get to the car to turn the ride down. While you're still safely in reach of a phone, explain that you don't need a ride after all because you've already ordered a cab/you just remembered that your parents offered to pick you up/you'd like a bit of a walk to get some fresh air/anything! Say anything at all! But don't get in! And if you have to be rude, be rude. It's worth it.

Chapter

At Home 5

The whole idea of protecting yourself at home is sort of depressing, isn't it ? After all, we all feel that our home should be the safest place in the world, and we shouldn't even have to *think* about the possibility of anything bad happening there, on our territory. In a way, though, that's just the point: We have every right to think of home as the place where nothing bad is going to happen to us. That's why it makes sense to do everything we can to make sure that it is always the safe place that we want it to be.

SECURITY AT HOME

In a way, your home is like a fortress—it keeps you and the people you care about safely inside, and scary people out—at least that's the general idea. It's funny, though: Some people just don't like that concept at all. Just stop any sweet old lady at a supermarket checkout and bring the subject up (if you've got about three hours to spare and are prepared to have your eardrums go into meltdown) and you're likely to get a rant along the lines of: "Oooh, in the old days, we used to leave our front door unlocked and our back door wide open and all our valuables hanging off the washing line and leave out big signs saying 'just popped out for two hours' and wander around in the nude with all the curtains open and you never had to worry a bit and isn't it terrible, English muffins have gone up by 10 cents again."

To be fair, there is some truth there (and I don't mean the bit about English muffins). Life *did* used to be somewhat safer and you didn't have to take as many precautions as you do today. But if you go further back, way back—think cavemen, think medieval castles—it's clear that the idea of protecting yourself and your home is nothing new. It has always made sense. Now, I'm not suggesting that we all stand guard by our front doors wielding clubs and sticks, or install arrow-slits and nifty devices to shower boiling oil on unwanted visitors. I'm just saying that if you can get used to the idea of seeing your home as your castle, it doesn't seem at all weird to do everything you can to make sure that everyone and everything inside it is completely safe from the outside world. After all, back in medieval times, people would have thought you were stark raving mad if you had a nice, potentially safe castle but, say, you answered the door to any old stranger who turned up, chirping: "Ooh sorry, everyone's partying down at the bar, so I'm all on my own!"

You get the point. So here's everything you need to know about staying safe at home.

Get equipped

"I used to think it was really good that we had the kind of lock on our front door that you could open with a credit card, because I'm always forgetting my keys and I would've been locked out so many times, otherwise. Then one day my friend was with me and I'd forgotten my keys again, and when she saw how I got in, she said we

were crazy, because if we could get in that way, so could a burglar. I couldn't believe we hadn't thought of it before, and I made my mom get some new locks the next day."

Marina, 17

"Our next door neighbors on both sides have been burgled, and we never have, knock wood. I'm sure that it's because we've got a burglar alarm and one of those lights that comes on whenever anyone comes near the house."

Alice, 15

These are the things that every home should have, no two ways about it:

• Strong door locks. You should preferably have more than one (of the kind you use keys with), plus a deadbolt—that's a big, super-mega version of the kind you find in public toilet stalls, which you lock from the inside—to keep locked when you're indoors.

• A door chain.

• A peephole in the front door.

• A light outside the front door. If your family or roommates are worried about the added electricity costs, it's worth buying the kind with a sensor that switches the light on automatically when someone is nearby and stays off the rest of the time.

• Good locks on the windows. Your family might also want to think about investing in a burglar alarm. The basic kind of alarm is one that goes off when someone opens or tampers with the door or windows from the outside. For a bit more cash, you can also get things like sensors which can detect people moving about inside the house (in case someone manages to fiddle with the window or door sensors and get in unnoticed) and panic buttons (which you put by the front door to use if someone tries to force their way in, or by the bed, in case you hear an intruder at night). You can also get your alarm system wired up to the local police station, which gives you the security of knowing that if your alarm goes off, the boys in blue will automatically be on their way over.

If you can't afford any kind of alarm, it's worth thinking about buying a fake alarm box to install outside your house—it looks just like the real thing, and is often enough to put burglars off.

Get smart

"I saw this film where a woman opened the front door and some bad guys burst in. I had bad dreams about it for ages, and I never open the door unless I know exactly who's there."

Claudette, 14

"My friend's mom and dad spent a fortune on getting all new locks and a burglar alarm fitted after they got burgled, then they never bothered using them. They got burgled again, and I'm not surprised. The insurance company found out that they'd gone out and left the window open and not set the alarm, and now they might not pay for all the stuff that got stolen. My friend is really

upset because she lost her stereo. It's the most stupid thing I've ever heard."

Jo, 14

Good, sturdy hardware counts for a lot, but common sense is just as important. Here are some basic precautions to remember:

- Always use what you have: there's no point in having window locks, a door chain, an alarm, etc. if you don't use them.

- Always keep your keys safe, and never give them to anyone you don't trust 100 percent.

- Avoid hiding keys outside your home—especially in obvious places like under a doormat or flower pot. If you don't have enough sets of keys to go around, or someone in your family is always misplacing theirs, it's definitely worth the expense of getting a spare set cut! And if you *must* leave keys out, it's far better to leave them with a neighbor, if you can.

- If you lose your keys (or anyone else who lives with you loses theirs), it's always sensible to get the locks changed. Of course, it can be mighty annoying to go through the expense and hassle only to have the keys turn up down the back of the couch two days later, but as the cliché goes, it's better to be safe than sorry.

- If you have a burglar alarm, don't tell *anyone* the code for switching it off. If you have to tell someone so they can use it, make sure no one else can overhear.

If you go away on vacation, or even for a short break, don't leave any clues that you're away. Always make sure that newspaper, milk, or any other regular deliveries are canceled, and that someone asks a neighbor to keep an eye on your place and make sure all your mail is picked up.

• If you have an answering machine, don't leave a message on it saying you're not home—it's better to say "we can't come to the phone right now," or something like that which sounds as if you could be in, otherwise it's like advertising that your home is empty.

• Don't forget that some creeps look out for signs of a female living alone, so if you do, or you live with just your mom, don't let them find any. The most common danger areas are the phone book and the labels by the doorbells in apartments.

• Never open the front door unless you know exactly who is behind it. You should always ask who is there, and if you have a peephole, use it every time you answer the door. If you live in an apartment that has an intercom system (so visitors start out downstairs, rather than right outside your door), never buzz them up unless you're utterly certain that the person ringing is no threat to you.

• If you're visited by a stranger who claims to be representing an organization (i.e., collecting for charity, canvassing for a political party, delivering something, doing a survey, checking the gas meter, whatever) think carefully. If you're home alone, you may feel safer not opening the door at all, just in case. Of course, you shouldn't tell a visitor that you're alone. Instead you could say that you can't answer the door right now because you're in the middle of something, and ask them to come back later (when someone else will be home).

• Even when you're not alone, you shouldn't automatically open the door. First of all, you should ask to see some identification—all of the people mentioned above should be carrying a proper ID card, with their picture, their name, and the name of the organization they represent printed on it. Ask them to hold it up to the peephole (if you have one) or if you have a door chain, leave it on and open the door far enough for the visitor to show you his or her card. If the card looks genuine, the person at your door looks like the person in the picture and your instincts tell you that everything is okay, then go ahead and open up.

Remember that it's not rude to ask to see someone's ID, and no one will be surprised or miffed—not even a police officer. It's worth mentioning here that some delivery people don't carry ID—particularly people from local stores. If that's the case, and you don't feel comfortable answering the door, you can always ask them to leave the goods outside the front door for you.

• If you decide to open the door to someone and you need to go off for any reason (maybe to get some cash if they're collecting for charity, or to fetch someone else who lives with you), always shut the door. If you're worried about seeming rude, say: "I hope you don't mind if I close the door, but I don't want my cat to get out." (Of course, it doesn't matter if you don't really have a cat—they don't know that, do they!)

Preparing for the Worst

"Our neighbor came by in a panic, saying she'd gotten home from work and her front door was hanging off, and she called the police from our place. They came right away, and you know what: The burglar was still in there! So it was just as well she didn't go in."

Stephanie, 16

"I think it's very bad that in films and television programs you often see people tricking burglars and attackers—you know, untying themselves and sneaking up and fighting with them. I'll bet if you tried that in real life you'd probably get hurt or maybe even killed. It definitely wouldn't work anyway. I'd rather let someone take all our valuables and not get hurt. Films shouldn't make out like it's always so easy to be a hero when it's not true."

Yumiko, 14

If you always take precautions, you shouldn't need to worry about anything bad happening. Still, it's always worth knowing the right thing to do, if the unthinkable ever happens.

• Never go into your house if you come home to discover any signs that you may have been broken into, especially if you're alone—there's always a chance that the intruder might still be there. If you've already gone in and found the suspicious signs inside, get out again, pronto. Either way, the thing to do is go swiftly to a neighbor's place or a nearby store or pay phone and call the police.

• If you're at home and you think you can hear an

intruder, the most important thing to do is protect yourself. Of course, not all burglars are violent, and many will run off as soon as they find out that there's someone home, but there's no way of telling who you're up against, so it would be crazy to take risks. Forget about confronting the intruder. Your number one goal is to keep yourself safe, which will allow you to achieve your second goal—to get help. First off, if you're in a room with a lock on the door, lock yourself in—it buys you some time to calm yourself down, gather your wits about you and try to think straight. Ideally, you want to get out of the house quickly and call the police from somewhere else. If you don't think you can do that safely (don't even consider getting out through a window unless you're on the ground floor), the next best thing is to call the police from inside your home. If there is no phone in the room you're in, and you don't think you can safely and quietly get to a lockable room with a phone in it (or you don't *have* a lockable room with a phone in it) you should try to get help by attracting attention from a window. Otherwise, just sit tight and stay safe—and if you can't lock the door, hide. Once you're certain that the intruder has left, call the police.

• If you find yourself confronted by an intruder in your home, you should never put up a fight. As I said before, it could well be that the intruder gets the fright of their life and scatters, but if not, you should avoid doing anything risky. Always be as calm, quiet, and cooperative as possible, and that counts double if the intruder has a weapon or appears to be violent or a bit weird and spaced out (he could be on drugs, which could make him extra nervous, and therefore more dangerous and unpredictable).

• Don't have nightmares—violent crime is very rare indeed, thank goodness.

SECURITY AWAY FROM HOME

Luckily, most hotels and vacation homes or apartments are pretty secure places. But it's still silly to take risks. Here are the essential vacation rules:

• Just like at home, you should never answer the door unless you know exactly who is there. If it's a hotel or apartment complex employee or a vacation rep, and you're alone and nervous, don't be afraid to ask them to come back later—you don't have to let them in.

• Don't forget to lock and/or bolt the door at night—use whatever security measures are there.

• It can be tempting to leave windows or balcony doors open at night, especially if you're somewhere hot, but it's not a great idea—unless, of course, you're on a high floor of a high-rise building, in which case no one could get in. Ideally, you should close and lock windows and balcony doors before you go to bed—most hotels in hot countries have air conditioning or fans to keep you cool.

• Don't leave valuables (money, travelers checks, jewelry, watches, cameras, and video cameras) in your hotel room, apartment, or villa during the day while you're out. Most hotels and some apartment complexes have safety deposit boxes (sometimes in the room), so use them. Otherwise, keep your valuables with you.

PHONE SENSE

One thing our medieval cousins didn't have to bother about was the phone. Once you were indoors, you were safe. Nowadays, you can have enough locks and bolts to put Fort Knox to shame, but if you think about it, the outside world can still sneak in through that little curly cord. Of course, the phone is basically a very nice thing, which only serves to make life easier and more fun. Make sure that it stays that way. For starters, it makes sense to take a few precautions to keep your phone number as private as possible. For instance:

• Don't give it to people you don't know or trust, even if they ask for it and you don't want to be rude (you could always tell them it's just been changed, and you can't remember the new number).

• If you need to advertise in a local paper, store window or bulletin board, why not ask a parent, relative, or older friend who works in an office if you can put their work number on the ad instead, and have them take the messages for you? If you can't do that, put only your number on the ad, not your name.

• Don't answer your phone by saying your phone number. Although it's unlikely, it's worth bearing in mind that if the person on the other end of the line was a dishonest caller, calling numbers at random, your reminder could give them a chance to make a note of yours and call you again in the future.

• If a caller asks what number they've just dialed, don't

tell them. Ask instead what number they were after, so that you can tell them whether they've called a wrong number or not. If they won't tell you what number they've dialed, hang up.

Unwanted calls

"I got a dirty phone call once. The man was saying such disgusting things, and I wanted to put the phone down, but it was like I was frozen to the spot. Afterward I couldn't stop crying."

India, 14

"The phone would ring, you'd answer it, and the person wouldn't say anything at all. It happened all the time, for about a year. My mom and dad just thought it was annoying, and told me not to worry about it, and my friends couldn't understand why I was upset, either. They said it wasn't like we were getting heavy breathing or something. I think it was just the fact that someone had our number, and was picking on us. I kept imagining that I could see someone following me. In the end, I went to the school counselor, and she was so great. I don't think I could have coped without her. It was great to talk to someone about it who didn't think I was being stupid."

Anastasia, 15

"I used to work at a well-known teenage girl's magazine, and we once had a call from this woman who told us that a man claiming to be from the magazine had phoned her daughter. Apparently this guy had told her that she had won a competition and told her to meet him at a local train station. I don't know if it was someone playing

a prank on the girl or some weirdo, but we were all so relieved that her mom had called to check. It made me feel quite sick, just thinking about what could have happened."

Sarah, 28

Unfortunately, it's not always possible to avoid getting unwanted calls. Read on for everything you need to know about them, and what to do about them:

- Suspiciously nosy calls

If a caller you don't know asks for your address, never give it to them, no matter who they claim to be. If they say that they know your parents, or someone else who lives with you, offer to take their name and number and have that person call them back later. Don't be too easily taken in by someone who says they're from some organization or delivery service and they're "checking" your address. Ask them what address they have listed for you—if it's right, or nearly right, and they don't sound especially risky, you can tell them they're correct. If they have it very wrong or they won't tell you, say that you can't help them, and hang up.

- Possible con calls

Never agree to meet someone you don't know who has called you on the phone and asked you to meet them for *any* reason. If you're convinced that they sound genuine, ask for their name and number so that your parents or another adult can speak to them later and check them out. Bear in mind that people from magazines, companies, and organizations simply would not do this, and it's far more likely to be a prank call or worse.

• Wrong numbers

Wrong numbers happen to everyone now and again. But if the same person seems to keep calling your number "by mistake," it's annoying and a bit spooky. Of course, it's always possible that the person is just really stupid, so first try saying in a firm, assertive tone of voice: "Look, you keep calling here but this is *not* the number you want. Please don't call again." If they call again after that, it's worth taking action (see page 87).

• Silent calls (when someone repeatedly phones and says nothing) and hang-ups (when someone calls and just hangs up right away)

These two kinds of calls are surprisingly nasty to receive. It's hard to explain to people who haven't experienced this kind of harassment just how unsettling it feels. Unlike other kinds of disturbing phone calls, which usually come from strangers or acquaintances who have a big problem, the culprit behind silent calls and hang-ups is quite often someone you've had a fight with or who has decided to pick on you—an ex-friend or ex-boyfriend or girlfriend, an enemy, or a bully. It is always worth taking action over these sorts of calls (see page 87).

• Prank calls

These are usually harmless but annoying, and they normally happen only once, unless they're part of a harassment "campaign" by someone you don't get along with. The less you say, the less fun it is for the caller, and if you don't react at all, they're unlikely to bother doing it again. If prank calls keep on coming, take action (see page 87).

- Heavy-breathing calls

These normally come from deeply sick people who would like to be making obscene or threatening calls but don't have the guts. You should always take action over these calls (see below).

- Obscene calls

Getting an obscene phone call is a horrible, horrible experience, and afterward you can feel shaken, frightened, upset, and sort of dirty, almost as if you'd been attacked. You should always hang up on an obscene caller right away, and you should always take action (see below). If the suggestions below don't work, and the calls keep coming, you should call the police for advice. You should also call the police if the caller seems to know you and suggests that he can see you or has been watching or following you, or the things he says are at all menacing or threatening.

- Menacing or threatening calls

If you get a menacing call of any kind—anything from someone telling you to "watch out" or saying something bad is going to happen to you, to someone talking about nasty, violent things or actually threatening you—you should call the police right away and also take the actions listed below.

Taking action over unwanted calls

You shouldn't have to put up with unwanted calls and being harassed in your own home over the telephone. Most telephone companies have new services designed to help you find out who made the last call to your number. You can get a caller identification box which displays the number of the person who is calling you. You can use the call return service, which lets you call back the last number that called you. All you do is dial the star key and 69. You might want your parents to do this for you since you might not know what to say if you do get that person on the line. There is also a call trace service for annoying, obscene, or harassing calls. If you receive a call, hang up, and then dial the star key and 57 and stay on the line. This will record your number, the caller's number, and the date and time the call was made. Though you will not be able to get the caller's number, this information can be passed on to the police by the phone company. Check with your local phone company to make sure these services are available in your area. And before you do anything mentioned above, check with your parents or another adult about what to do with the information you get.

If the calls you're getting are just a bit of a nuisance, it might be worth getting an adult to call the number to try to find out who is making the calls, and warn them to stop. Threats probably won't be necessary—the sheer embarrassment of being found out is usually enough to put a stop to the caller's fun and games. If the calls you're getting are nasty enough to have persuaded you to call the police, though, you can give the police the number and *they* will decide what to do next.

These phone services are certainly going to put a stop to a lot of unwanted calls. But if the number turns out to belong to someone you know, you might feel too embarrassed to let someone call them back. Or what if the person at the number you're given is a stranger who claims to know nothing about the calls and says it must be someone else who uses that number? And, of course, if your area doesn't have the services, you won't have the choice anyway. Don't worry—there *are* other solutions for putting a stop to unwanted calls. Following these steps usually does the trick:

- Remember that most unwanted callers are after an audience at the very least, and, better still, a big reaction to what they are doing. The more you say (particularly if you get wound up or upset) the more interesting and satisfying the whole experience is for the caller. Never encourage a caller by talking to them, not even to insult them. If you say nothing and simply hang up as soon as you realize that the call is an unwanted one, the caller is likely to lose interest fairly quickly, with any luck.

- If the calls carry on, the caller is obviously getting enough of a kick just from hearing you say hello and knowing that you must be feeling uncomfortable and unhappy about the calls. (Aren't some people awful?) So the next step is to stop answering the phone. If you live with your dad or another adult man, have him answer it instead, every time. If you have an answering machine, you should also have him record a message so that you can leave the machine on when he is out or unable to get to the phone. You'll be able to hear people talking on the machine, so you and the other members of your household can pick up the calls you want to take. If you don't have a man around the house, just ask a man you know to do the message and leave the answering machine on *all the time*.

• If you don't have an answering machine, this would certainly be a very good time to invest in one. Failing that, you could ask a friend or relative to lend you theirs until the calls have stopped—if you explain what's going on, they're bound to want to help out.

• If you can't get your hands on an answering machine, or the other people you live with won't agree to having it on all the time, try this: keep a loud whistle by the phone. Try to get the kind that hikers and mountaineers use to attract attention when they're in trouble—they're the loudest. You can buy them from most sports and camping shops. When your caller calls again, grab the whistle and let it rip. It's quite an ear bashing, and only a real glutton for punishment would call again and risk a second helping!

• If neither the answering machine nor the whistle do the trick, it's time to scare your caller a bit. Get someone else—preferably a guy—to put on a professional-sounding serious voice and record you a new answering machine message, saying this: "For reasons of security, all calls to this number are being recorded and traced. If you would like to have your call returned, please leave your message after the tone."

• If all the above fail, contact your phone company. There are various other services that can block or restrict calls to your number. In some cases the caller will get a message saying that the call will not be accepted unless the restriction is removed. This works in the case of caller identification services when the caller is blocking his or her number from being identified. You can have your number restricted so that it cannot appear on someone else's caller identification. You can also call your operator to ask for advice on what services you can use to protect your telephone privacy.

- You can also ask the phone company to give you a new phone number.

Holding it all together

If you've never had an experience with unwanted calls, you might not think that they'd be all that distressing, especially in comparison with other kinds of attack or harassment. You'd be pretty wrong—unwanted calls can make you feel frightened and shaky, and leave you feeling utterly miserable for a long time afterward, unable to stop thinking about them. Don't keep your feelings in. You should always tell your friends, parents, and anyone else you trust what's up, and let them help you cope with the trauma by talking things through with you. Being on the receiving end of unwanted calls is not your fault, and nothing to be ashamed of, so you should never suffer through this situation alone, in secret.

CHAIN LETTERS

It's amazing how upsetting it can be to get a chain letter which tells you that something horrible will happen to you if you break the chain. But the fact is that chain letters are stupid, superstitious nonsense. They're a waste of paper, a waste of a stamp, and a waste of everybody's time. Take it from me, nothing bad has *ever* happened to *anyone* as a result of breaking a chain letter.

The scary stories which are sometimes written on chain letters as examples of things that have happened to people who broke the chain are just out and out, made-up lies. If you receive a chain letter, put it right in the garbage where it belongs.

PEEPING TOMS

"I looked out of my window and saw the boy who lives across the street looking right at me, with a pair of binoculars. I nearly died. I suppose I didn't know whether he had ever done it before, and I couldn't remember if I'd ever gotten undressed with the curtains open, but I was so upset. He goes to my school, and I pretended to be sick for two weeks so I wouldn't have to go in and face him. The thought of it made me feel ill."

Ann, 16

"My sister is a nurse and they had a Peeping Tom who was hanging around the nurses' quarters. They only found out about him because he used to climb up this tree to get a good view, and one night he fell out of the tree and broke his leg! They heard him yelling for help, and when they asked what he was doing in the tree, he was really embarrassed. They called the police on him, and bandaged up his leg while they were waiting. My sister said they felt sorry for him, because he was just a stupid, dirty old man, but I think what he did was disgusting, and I'm glad he broke his leg. If I were them, I would have left him to suffer."

Corinne, 14

Unfortunately, it occasionally turns out that even if your home is totally secure, someone can still invade your privacy. A Peeping Tom is a person—usually a man—who gets a kick out of secretly spying on people who are getting undressed, wandering around in the nude, or getting intimate with someone else.

I always think Peeping Tom is a name that is far too friendly and harmless-sounding for what is actually a person with a very nasty, calculated habit that can make the poor, unsuspecting people they spy on feel really quite spooked and violated. The proper name for this habit is voyeurism, and if a voyeur spies on you, he is breaking the law.

Obviously, the best way to make sure that you never become a victim of a voyeur is to make sure that you keep your curtains and blinds closed, especially when you're getting undressed or doing something private. You should do this even if you think that your window can't possibly be seen through anyone else's window.

Peeping Toms are often so driven by their habit that they'll go out of their way to watch people, and they sometimes use binoculars. You should also make sure that your curtains and blinds aren't at all see-through. If you can see anything through them, then you can bet for sure that someone on the other side can see through them too. Even if you can't see out, it's possible that someone else can see in, especially when it's dark outside and you have your lights on. It's not a bad idea to switch your light on and run outside to check it out. And, of course, if people can see in, you should improve your window coverings—have a thicker lining put in your curtains (or just hang a sheet or towel from the rail behind them), and add curtains where a blind isn't doing it's job.

It can be very scary to spot someone watching you through your window, and if you discover that you have been a victim of a Peeping Tom, you have every right to go to the police and tell them about it. Rest assured, though, that voyeurs are hardly ever dangerous. On the whole, they're wimpy, sad creeps who just like to look—so you shouldn't let yourself feel scared that you're in any kind of physical danger. Still it's a very nasty feeling to think that a horrible stranger has seen you without your clothes on, or doing something private, and, as with all unpleasant experiences, it's very important to share your feelings. Talk things through with someone you trust so that you can start feeling happy and safe again and get on with your life.

ABUSE IN THE HOME

"You wouldn't believe how many of my friends have been abused. I don't think people know exactly how much it goes on."

Alana, 17

We've talked about keeping nasty people safely outside your home, but the saddest fact of all is that sometimes the very person you most need protection from is already in there, with you. I'm talking about abuse—sexual, physical, or both, and it happens far, far more than people realize.

Every year, thousands of kids and teenagers get hurt, felt up, forced into sexual acts, and raped by the very people who are supposed to be protecting and caring for them—parents, stepparents, foster parents, workers in children's homes. Thousands more are abused by other relatives, their parents' live-in partners, and trusted family friends. Some abusers are violent, some make threats, others try to persuade their victims that what they are doing is not wrong, and all abusers take advantage of the power they have as adults.

No matter who is doing the abusing, these facts remain the same: what they are doing is evil, illegal, and utterly inexcusable. To be abused by someone you should rightly expect to be loving, protecting, and trustworthy is one of the most tragic, devastating things that can happen to anyone.

If you are being abused, it is extremely important to understand that *you* haven't done anything wrong. The victim is *never* to blame for what happens to them, and yet so many victims of abuse feel guilty. No one deserves to be abused, and no matter how you react in a situation where you're being abused (whether you don't put up a fight, whether you maybe even experience sexual feelings that aren't entirely unpleasant) you are not responsible for what has happened to you. If you have feelings of guilt, try to fight them, because you have *nothing* to feel guilty about. Concentrate on feeling angry with your abuser instead, and determined to protect yourself and set things right.

The most important thing to do if you have been abused is to tell someone about it. You don't have to decide right away whether you want to involve the police. The first and most important step is to reach out and share your painful secret with someone else so that you can start getting your life in order. Choose a responsible adult who you trust. If you're afraid to tell a parent or guardian (perhaps because the abuser is someone close to them), choose another older relative, a teacher you like, or your doctor. If you can't think of anyone you'd feel comfortable talking to, or you think you might prefer to talk to someone you don't know, there are plenty of people available, just waiting at the other end of a telephone line whenever you want them—kind, friendly, professional counselors who will totally understand your problem and be prepared to get involved as much or as little as you want. They are there to lend an ear, encourage you to talk things through, answer your questions, give you support and advice, help you decide what to do next and even help you to take legal action, if that's what you decide that you want to do. You'll find their numbers at the end of this book.

Even if you decide for yourself right from the start that you want to involve the police, it's a good idea to get the support of a social worker or a help-line counselor, because they can tell you exactly what to expect at each stage in the process.

Chapter 6
At School

In theory, school is somewhere that you can be safe and off guard. You're among people you know, you're shut off from the outside world, and there are plenty of adults around who, although they might be annoying at times, are basically looking out for you and have your best interests at heart.

Unlike most everyday situations, though, where usually you can take a handful of sensible precautions to make sure that nothing unpleasant happens to you, school is a slightly different area. If you think about it, there isn't a lot of choice involved—you have to go there, you have to go to classes, and (unless you're allowed out of school at break times) you pretty much know exactly where you're going to be and what you're going to be doing all day long. The bottom line is that you can't avoid going to school, and therefore if you find yourself in a difficult situation at school, there wouldn't have been much you could have done to avoid it in the first place. The key, then, is to deal with nasty situations as soon as they happen so that you can go to school without fear of anything bad happening again.

BULLYING

Being bullied is an incredibly unpleasant experience, and anyone who doesn't take it seriously has obviously never experienced it personally. The suffering you go through as a victim of bullying goes way beyond the pain of being hurt, the upset of being insulted, or the horrible dread of turning up at school every day wondering what the bully will do next: You might feel bad about yourself because you're disliked, feel as if you've somehow let your family down, feel angry that other people aren't doing anything to stop this hideous thing from happening to you.

Bullying goes on in schools because people allow it to go on. It's not only the fault of the losers who do the bullying. Think about the victims who don't tell on bullies, the people who know that bullying is going on but don't do anything about it, the teachers who believe that because bullying has always gone on in schools, it always will. Basically, bullies know that they have a good chance of getting away with the things they do, and in a way we're all to blame for that. Read on to find out what do if you're a victim of a bully, and what *you* can do about putting a stop to bullying for good—at your school, at every school, for ever.

Sticks and stones

"This girl used to call me names and make fun of me. I tried to ignore her, but I couldn't. It just really upset me. It got so bad that I didn't want to go to school, and I started making excuses, pretending to be sick all the time, or playing hooky. In the end it all caught up with me, and I had to tell my mom what was going on. She told the school—basically to get me out of trouble for skipping—and I don't know what they did, but the bullying stopped, anyway. It was such a relief, and I

wished that I'd told someone before, instead of suffering in silence for so long."

Nyra, 14

"I'd only just switched schools, and I could tell right away that she was the class bully. When she started on me—saying I was ugly and I smelled and stuff—I thought, if I let her get away with it, this is just going to go on and on. So I laughed in her face and told her: 'Have you looked in a mirror lately? You're not so gorgeous yourself!' Everyone laughed, and she never bothered me again after that. I suppose she only likes picking on people who are weaker than her. It helped make me some friends, as well."

Pritti, 14

Verbal abuse—being called names, being insulted, being teased, being made to feel embarrassed—can often be just as bad as being physically hurt.

People often suggest that you ignore a verbal bully, and although this can sometimes get them off your back, it can also encourage them to keep on trying more and more extreme ways to get a reaction from you. If you're dead certain that you can keep on ignoring a bully forever, no matter what they say or do, then fine. But in reality, it's difficult, because the chances are that eventually they're going to go far enough to make you snap—and then all the time and effort and self-control you spent ignoring them in the past will be wasted. Besides, who needs the hassle of some irritating jerk pestering you endlessly?

The best way to deal with a bully on your own is to prove to them that you're not prepared to be bullied.

Bullies tend to pick on people they think are vulnerable, so if you let a bully see that they have gotten to you, they're going to peg you as a perfect target. A bully is basically a loser who can only feel confident when they're making someone else feel small and afraid. You should try to stand up to bullies, although that doesn't mean getting into a fight with them. It would be silly to lower yourself to their level—you're far better than that. Instead, you should show the bully that you're confident, proud, and mature, and that you're just not at all interested in becoming the latest victim. The best thing to do when someone picks on you is look them in the eye and say something like: "You know, I really don't care what you think," then walk away.

If a bully refuses to leave you alone, there's only one thing to do: Tell on them. See *Reporting a bully* on page 101, for the lowdown.

When it goes beyond name-calling

"There were six or seven of them, and a couple of times they all laid into me so badly that I was covered in bruises—black eye, the works. I told my dad that I'd gotten it playing volleyball, but I could tell that he didn't believe me. Then I saw a program on television about a girl who had gotten in a fight with a bully and been stabbed, and she'd died, and I thought, I bet if she's looking down from somewhere now, she's thinking: I wish I'd never given the bully the chance. I reported everything the next day, and even though I can't say it was all over right away, he never touched me again, so I'm really glad I did it."

Kerry, 15

When an adult gets pushed around, kicked, punched, slapped, thumped, or injured in any other way by another person, there are all sorts of fancy, serious-sounding names for what has happened: grievous bodily harm, mugging, assault, battery. When a kid or teenager gets beaten up at school they call it bullying. Marvelous, isn't it? Don't buy this nonsense. *Every* physical attack should be taken as seriously as the next. If a stranger hurt you, would you shrug it off, keep it a secret, let them get away with it? Of course not. (At least, I hope you wouldn't!) See what I'm getting at? You should never ignore a physical attack by a bully, because it's just too important: No one has any right to lay a finger on you. This kind of bullying should always be reported right away.

Reporting a bully

"I was a bit scared after I reported her, especially when she passed me this note that said: 'You're gonna be sorry.' I thought, well, what have I got to lose now? I showed our teacher the note, and apparently she got into even more trouble because of that. The best part was seeing her going into the principal's office with her mom, looking all choked up. I'd always thought she was so mature and tough, and suddenly I realized that she wasn't."

Mai, 13

It's outrageous that there is so much stigma attached to reporting bullying. People talk about tattling on someone like it was a really wimpy thing to do, a real social no-no, and the whole idea of the "rules of the playground" (the unwritten law that says you shouldn't involve adults in your business) is just crazy. The whole thing was invented by bullies to protect themselves. Anyone who takes this to heart is guilty of protecting the bullies and making life easy for them. The truth is that reporting a bully doesn't mean that you're soft, or wimpy, or babyish. It actually proves that you have guts galore, you're self-confident enough to refuse to be bullied, and that you have the maturity and brains to figure out that the "rules of the playground" are a load of garbage.

Often the hardest part of reporting that you're being bullied is having your parents find out what's going on, if they don't know already. It's very common to feel that you'd rather they didn't know, because most of us want to make our parents happy, and we feel—whether rightly or wrongly—that they'd be upset to think that we were anything less than superpopular at school, or even that we were unhappy. Well, the fact is that bullying has precisely nothing to do with popularity. In every case, it's not the victim who has a problem getting along with people, but the bully. Anyway, every parent's major concern is that their kid is safe and happy, and that is going to be the main issue for them.

Another thing that puts many people off reporting bullying, or at least makes the decision harder for them, is the dread of what the bully might do in retaliation. Obviously the bully is not going to be thrilled about being in trouble, and yes, they may well get angry, but it doesn't automatically follow that the bullying will get worse. Usually, whatever punishment or warning they get will put them off going near you ever again. Of course, you can't get a cast-iron guarantee, but it's just not worth letting the fear put you off. If you don't tell, it means that (a) The bully has won; and (b) the bullying is going to carry on. You'll also find that once you've reported a bully, the feeling of relief is enormous.

It's worth bearing in mind that when you report a bully, you are doing *everyone* a favor—not just yourself. Bullies don't usually have just one victim; they keep on bullying until they are stopped. When you report a bully, you are doing it for everyone they have ever bullied, and everyone they ever would have bullied in the future.

Stamping out bullying for good

If bullying is ever going to stop, it's up to all of us to do our bit. So remember:

- Never let a bully get away with bullying you. Don't just hope it'll go away—report bullying.

- Never let a bully get away with bullying anyone else. No matter how scary the bully seems, no matter how relieved you are that it's not you getting picked on, have some guts and report what's going on.

- If you can't muster up enough guts to get yourself involved like that, make an effort to talk to the victim—even if they're not a friend of yours. Lend a sympathetic ear, then persuade them that reporting the bully is the right thing to do.

- If a bully is reported, but you don't feel that enough has been done about it, make it your job to complain. Remember that your school is being run for *your* benefit. In a way, the teachers and principal are working for you, and if what they're doing isn't up to scratch, you have every right to complain to them about it. Obviously, though, you shouldn't get pushy with a teacher or principal—not just because it's disrespectful, but because you won't get results. And of course, if you get in trouble yourself for being difficult, you'll be out of the game, and you're far too valuable in the fight against bullying to afford for that to happen. Instead, ask a teacher or your principal if you can see them in private (take a friend or a group of friends with you, if you like), and calmly and simply tell them that you don't feel that enough is being done about bullying.

If you're really serious about putting a stop to bullying

Why not form an antibullying committee with your friends? Here are some things you could do:

- Make a petition for other people in your class and the school to sign saying that they want bullying stopped for good. People shouldn't need much persuading to sign up, but if you want to help them understand just how serious bullying is, it might be worth going to the library and making copies of some newspaper clippings about teenagers and kids who have committed suicide because they were being bullied. There have also been some cases where violent bullying went too far, and victims have ended up in a hospital or even been killed in a situation that started as "just" bullying.

- Make up an antibullying charter to show to your principal. It should contain as many suggestions as you can think of that might help stop bullying. Some things you could suggest are:

1. Stricter punishments for *any kind* of bullying, maybe on a rigid warnings system (i.e., two warnings and you're automatically suspended, three and you're expelled).

2. Putting more teachers on duty at break times.

3. Setting up a reward system for people who report bullying—perhaps you could arrange an antibullying cake sale to raise funds, and use the proceeds to run the reward system. You could put a price of $5 on any bully's head, to be paid out when a bully is caught and stopped. If more than one person reports the bully, they would share the money (although the actual victim should always get a bigger share, if that was the case).

4. Making it official that bullying outside of school is considered school business, so that bullies can't get away with attacking their victims on the way to or from school.

5. Setting up a victim support team (possibly you and your friends?) so that victims of bullying know that they have a group of sympathetic people to talk to when they're going through the difficult experience of reporting a bully.

• Ask your teacher or principal to make an announcement about your antibullying committee, and any new rules, at assembly.

• Organize a survey team—pick one person to survey a class each—and do a regular monthly bullying survey. The team should talk in private to every member of the class they've been assigned to (ask your principal for a copy of every class register, so you can check the names off) and ask whether or not they have been bullied in the last few weeks. The question should make it clear that "bullying" includes being called names, teased, embarrassed, etc., not just being obviously taunted or hurt. Encourage people to answer truthfully, and instruct your team not to suddenly turn into the Spanish Inquisition if someone answers yes. If people are scared to answer yes, they might lie, and then the survey won't be accurate. Once you've tallied the results of your survey, they can be read out regularly at assembly.

- Once you've got your antibullying committee up and running, you could ask your teacher to help you contact a local paper and ask them to write an article about you. With any luck, other schools in your area would follow your example.

- If your efforts paid off and you managed to stamp out bullying in your school (and there's no reason why that shouldn't happen) you could start thinking much bigger. With the help of your teacher or principal, you could contact the national papers, and the Secretary of Education, telling them about what you have done, and suggesting that other schools throughout the country be made aware of what can be achieved with a bit of determination and hard work.

All that may seem like a lot of hassle, but it couldn't be more worthwhile. It would be terrible just to sit back and not get involved when you have the power to make such a difference. If every school in the country learned from what you did, if everyone got the message that no one is going to put up with bullying in schools any more, the day would come when no one would ever be bullied again. Wouldn't that be fantastic? And just think, you could go down in history, because it would have started with you.

SEXUAL HARASSMENT

Bullying is definitely the biggest problem in schools because it's so common. But now and again, sadly, other bad things happen.

Sexual harassment is one of those funny words that people use to mean all sorts of things—from the very serious (like sexual assault) to the kind of thing that one person might get very upset by and the next would happily ignore and forget about. That doesn't mean that the littler things are not serious, though—if you feel weird, embarrassed, or uncomfortable about something that someone does or says, then it's serious enough.

Harassment by other pupils often starts around the time of puberty. Raging hormones can make people say and do some pretty stupid things, and—particularly if you're in a coed school—you might be unfortunate enough to find yourself on the receiving end. Of course, having raging hormones doesn't give anyone the right to violate someone else's rights, and that's exactly what harassment is, even if the comment or action was originally meant just as a bit of fun or a joke.

Teachers should always know better than to harass a pupil in any way, but unfortunately, it sometimes happens. Some milder kinds of harassment—like making embarrassing personal comments—happen because a teacher wants to appear cool and "chummy," and they're too thoughtless to realize that their comments could be upsetting. Very occasionally, though, you get teachers who exploit their position of authority to harass their pupils, often knowing full well that what they're doing is deadly serious and utterly wrong.

Let's look at some of the different kinds of harassment, and what to do about them.

Personal comments

"Our English teacher is such a perv. He's always making really personal comments to all the girls. One day our class was getting books in the library and he told everyone to finish up quickly and sit down. My friend was up on a really high ladder next to him, and said 'Hang on!' He said: 'No hurry, Vickie, I'm enjoying the view!' Then she called him a dirty old man, as a joke, and he went and gave her detention for it. I didn't think that was fair—I didn't think that what she said was any worse than what he said. How come he's allowed to say whatever he wants but no one else can?"

Linda, 16

"When I started growing hair under my armpits, the boys all noticed at swimming. Three of them kept going on and on about it, and they kept saying they bet I had pubes as well. After that they shouted 'Show us your pubes!' every time I walked past. I ignored them, but I was so embarrassed. Honestly, I dreaded going in to school. It didn't help that my name rhymed with 'hairy,' either, as you can imagine!"

Mary, 18

Any personal comment of a sexual nature, no matter how it is meant, is harassment if it makes you feel uncomfortable. For instance a male teacher who looks at a girl pupil's breasts and says: "My, you've grown over summer vacation!" may have meant it to be funny, but the fact is that he's still commenting on something that is none of his business and putting the girl into an embarrassing situation. Similarly, a boy who yells: "Been shoplifting melons again?" might think he's said just about the funniest thing ever (although, let's face it, he's not exactly going to have David Letterman banging on his door begging for help with his scripts anytime soon), but if you're on the receiving end, it can be humiliating and horrible.

• Dealing with teachers who make personal comments
When a teacher makes an embarrassing remark, it often leaves you so shocked that you don't know what to say, so you don't say anything at all. If you're feeling brave, though, it's a good idea to say something like: "I don't think you should say things like that to your pupils." This gives the teacher the benefit of the doubt—if he was just messing around, it will hopefully bring it home to him that his little quip wasn't appropriate. If he was deliberately trying to embarrass you, or actually being disgusting, then it shows him that you're aware of what's right and what's wrong, and that you're not afraid to speak up. That alone should be enough of a threat to stop him from doing it again. Of course, saying "Get lost, you filthy old man!" might have the same effect, but it would get you into trouble, so forget it. If you're not rude, but your teacher gets angry anyway and threatens you (with detention, extra homework, whatever) you should calmly warn him that you don't think you were out of line, and that you are prepared to explain the whole thing to the principal and see what he or she thinks.

If a teacher frequently makes leery comments to you, even after you have made it clear that you are not happy about it, you should secretly make an appointment to see the principal and tell what is going on. It can be a hard thing to do, because on the one hand you do want the embarrassing comments to stop, but on the other, you don't want the teacher to pick on you in class as revenge. It can be doubly hard if the teacher is someone friendly that you're actually quite fond of, because there's the added fear that the teacher won't like you any more. It is *enormously* important to get over your worries and report this sort of thing, though, because: (a) No one has the right to embarrass or upset you, and it's up to you to stand up for your rights; and (b) if the teacher is genuinely unaware that he's doing something wrong, he needs to be told by someone he'll actually listen to: the principal. Besides, it's unlikely that the principal will use your name when talking to the culprit—especially if you ask him or her not to. Don't be afraid, either, that the principal won't believe you—harassment is taken very seriously these days, thank goodness.

• Dealing with other students who make personal comments
Ignoring comments will often put a stop to them, because it's often the victim's embarrassed reaction that makes the whole experience fun. However, the harasser may be getting a kick just from saying the things they say, or they might be doing it to impress their friends, in which case ignoring them probably won't make that much difference. The best plan is to stand up for yourself—show that you don't like being harassed—and then ignore any comments after that. Say whatever you like (I think: "Go away and don't bother speaking to me again until you've grown up," is a good one), but whatever you say, stay cool and

collected. Just make it clear that you're just not interested in hearing any more of this garbage.

If someone goes on and on and on, making comments whenever you walk past, it's a form of bullying. Quietly warn your harasser that if they don't stop bothering you, you're going to report them—and stick to your word. They probably won't get into that much trouble, but a teacher will tell them to leave you alone—which is exactly what you want.

Ultrapersonal comments and come-ons

"The afterschool tennis practice goes on until six and I was going to a party miles away at seven-thirty, so I figured I wouldn't bother going home first. I changed into all my gear—this little skirt and tight T-shirt—and put my makeup on in the bathroom, and when our gym teacher saw me, he looked me up and down and said: 'Lizzie, what can I say? If only you were a few years older....' I thought I was going to throw up."

Lizzie, 16

"The teacher had sent me to the closet to get some stuff and there was this sixth-grader in there already. He blocked the door and said: 'Sorry, but I'm afraid I can't let you out until I've screwed you!' I suppose he was joking—well I know he was, because he let me out after he'd said it—but the way he said it and the look on his face were horrible. For a minute it was like the scariest moment of my life."

Becky, 13

"I was getting my bags out of my locker and this boy from my class came up behind me and whispered: 'I had

a dream about you last night, and you were great in bed!' He said some other things as well which I don't even want to repeat. It was vile."

Robyn, 14

Some comments are just *way* too personal or disgusting to put up with at all, and, because they can be very upsetting, are a dead serious business.

• Dealing with teachers who make way too personal comments
Since teachers aren't supposed to be personal with you at all, they don't have to step that far over the mark before they're in shaky territory. For instance, if a teacher makes an ultra personal comment (like "You look tired! Had a long night with your boyfriend, did you?"), asks you an ultrapersonal question (like "Are you a virgin?") or gives you a creepy come-on, it is totally wrong. You should always report this kind of thing. Do it for yourself, because it is upsetting and nasty, and because you should always protect your rights, and do it for other people who may also be getting harassed by the same teacher and might not have the guts to report it themselves.

• Dealing with students who make way too personal comments
If someone makes a comment that is so personal or explicit that you feel disgusted or frightened (for instance telling you in great detail what they'd like to do to you, or telling you stuff about themselves that you really don't want to know), you should make it very clear to them that you don't like what they're saying.

Say whatever feels comfortable, whether it's "Shut up" or something more detailed. If someone won't stop making these comments you should report them to a teacher who can tell them in no uncertain terms to leave you alone. The same goes for someone who repeatedly asks you out or leers at you, even when you keep telling them that you're not interested. If someone's comments are very, very disgusting, or violent as well as sexual, they might have a problem, and by telling a teacher who may be able to help, you'd be doing *them* a favor too.

Accidental touching

"Our gymnastics teacher's catchphrase is: 'Backs straight!' He says it all the time, and he comes around and sets you straight. But I swear a few times he's touched our butts. My friend once said to him as a joke: 'That's not my back!' but he didn't seem to take any notice. So maybe he's doing it by accident after all."

Sherrie, 14

"In drama, we were learning how to pretend to faint. We had to go in pairs and take turns for one to faint and the other to catch them. You were meant to catch the other person under their arms. I was in a pair with this boy, and when he caught me, he put his hands on my boobs instead of under my arms but I was too embarrassed to say anything."

Kira, 13

Accidental touching can be a tricky area, because it's often difficult to work out exactly what is going on. It can sometimes be hard, for instance, to tell whether someone who has brushed against you did so on purpose or by accident. And is a teacher just being friendly when he puts his arm around you, or what? Use good judgment: If someone brushes against you when they walk past, and they didn't have much room, it was probably an accident. If they had tons of room, or it would have been easier for them to go another way around, it may well not have been an accident at all. If the person has harassed you in the past, in other ways (i.e., by making comments), you should be more suspicious. Similarly, if someone puts an arm around you, the chances are that it's just being friendly. If the arm seems to be resting on your butt or breast, it's a bit suspicious, and it wouldn't be out of order to suspect that it was no accident.

• Dealing with a teacher who accidentally touches you
Most teachers are, quite rightly, very careful about making physical contact with their pupils because they know that they could get into big trouble over touching a student, even if it really was an accident. So if a teacher accidentally touches your butt or breasts, they're either very stupid and careless, or it wasn't an accident at all. No one has any right to touch you without your consent, and it is very, very serious and very, very foul when an adult who is in a position of authority violates this right. The problem with those "was-it-my-imagination?" situations is that a teacher can quite easily claim that it was all your imagination even if it wasn't. If you're absolutely sure, stand by your convictions and report it. Otherwise you could try talking to others to see if they have had similar experiences. If they have, then the chances are that what happened to you wasn't just your

imagination, and maybe you can all report the incidents to the principal together.

• Dealing with another student who accidentally touches you

The best thing you can do is steer clear of the offender to avoid anything happening again—that's if the touch *was* done on purpose. If someone seems to be going out of their way to get near you and accidentally touch you quite often, it's worth giving them a dirty look or telling them to leave you alone, to show them that you know what they're up to. If this doesn't work, report them, so that a teacher can tell them to stay away—that should do the trick.

Touching

"Every time they cut the grass on the playing field at our school, everyone would have a big grass fight. It was a lot of fun. But one time, it turned into a groping free-for-all, with a huge gang of boys leaping on one girl at a time, pretending to stuff grass down her clothes, but actually taking the opportunity to cop a feel. When I look back, it's incredible to think of the way it was all seen as no big deal. The teachers didn't even notice and the boys thought it was all a huge laugh. I didn't get attacked because I locked myself in the bathroom, but my friends who did were pretty shaken up. They never dreamed of reporting it, though, because they didn't want to be seen as being uptight or as having no sense of humor. I often think, though, that if you told this story leaving out the facts that it happened at a school and started as a grass fight, it would sound so serious, so terrible: twenty or so guys jumping on a girl, holding her down, and touching

her breasts and privates. It doesn't sound at all like 'a bit of fun' when you tell it that way. I realize now how awful it actually was."

Talisa, 21

I'm talking here about touching that *definitely* isn't an accident—when someone touches, feels, pats, grabs, strokes, prods, squeezes, pinches, or gropes you, especially in an intimate area (like your butt or boobs, or between your legs). If someone touches you in any of those ways when you don't want them to, it is basically sexual assault, and that's a very serious thing indeed.

- Dealing with a teacher who touches you

A teacher who touches you in any of the ways mentioned above should not be working in a school—period. If a teacher does something like that to you, he may or may not be planning on going any further, but you should always pull away and shout "No!" loudly, to make it clear that you are aware of what he has just done, and that it is not at all okay by you. No matter how small the assault—even if it's "just" a pinch on the butt or something—you're likely to feel very upset, shaky, and weird. This is all perfectly normal, but it's essential that you don't keep it all in. You need to tell someone else what has happened (a friend, a parent, anyone), for your own sake, and you also need to report the teacher so that he doesn't get the opportunity to assault you or anyone else, ever again. Rest assured that your accusation will be taken very, very seriously, and that you can expect to be treated sympathetically.

• Dealing with a student who touches you

It's quite amazing how often groping and grabbing goes on in coed schools, and how the people doing the touching often don't realize that what they're doing is assault, and how wrong and how serious it is. Often their victims don't fully realize how seriously they have been violated, either. The point is that you should never accept anything that happens to you just because it happens at school, or it starts out as a joke, or you're worried about what people will think of you. If you think that someone has done something wrong to you, never be afraid to report it.

Sexual assault

Very, very rarely, major sexual assaults and rapes do happen in schools. The fact that they happen in schools, and that the attacker is someone that the victim knows, is beside the point—it's assault or rape, just the same. See Chapter Seven for everything you should know about these serious crimes.

Chapter 7 Coping with Crime

FLASHERS

"I was walking through the park to get to school and I could see this old man walking toward me. It was only when he got closer that I saw he had his penis hanging out of his pants. I just screamed. I wanted to run right away, but it was like I was frozen to the spot for a while. When I got to school I was shaking and felt sick all day. I kept thinking about it, and I felt really embarrassed that I didn't run right away: I thought the man must have thought I wanted to look at his penis. In the end my teacher could tell that something was wrong so I told her and she was great. She called the police for me, too."

Leonie, 14

"This boy sat behind me on the bus—he wasn't that old—and he was making all these panting noises. I suppose I shouldn't have looked around, but I didn't think about it. Anyway, he was playing with his thing. I just turned around and pretended I hadn't seen. I didn't want to tell any of my friends afterward, because last year one of my friends got flashed and she wasn't bothered at all—she said she'd shouted something at the guy like: 'Sorry I haven't got a microscope!' because his penis was really small, and we'd all been laughing about it. I told my mom a few weeks later, and she said not to feel bad—she said that everyone deals with

things in different ways, and that my friend was probably as upset as me, she just showed it in a different way. I felt much better after that, but I still didn't tell anyone else."

Tamika, 16

A flasher is someone who shows their private parts to other people. Flashers are almost always male, and they usually do it because they get off on people looking at them, and the reactions they get. Most often, flashers just expose themselves, although you sometimes get flashers who masturbate in public, too.

Being the victim of a flasher can be very shocking and disturbing, but it's pretty reassuring to know that flashers are rarely dangerous—they're sad and sick, but they're not going to hurt anyone physically. However, there *are* a small percentage of flashers who *can* be dangerous. Research has turned up an interesting fact: if a flasher's penis is limp, he is almost certainly going to be the harmless type; if his penis is erect (hard and sticking out) there is a higher chance that he could be violent. While this fact is interesting, and can be a comfort if you've been flashed by someone with a limp penis (at least you can tell yourself that, however nasty the experience, you weren't in any danger), it obviously makes sense to get as far away as possible from *any flasher*, as fast as you can—there's no sense in sticking around any longer than you have to.

Flashing is illegal—the crime itself is called *indecent exposure*—and the police take it very seriously indeed. If you're the victim of a flasher, you should always file a report. Even if the incident didn't bother you that much, you should do it because the flasher desperately needs help putting a stop to his vile habit, and for the sake of other victims he might confront in the future if he's not stopped—people who might be deeply, deeply disturbed for life by the experience.

You should also be sure to talk to your close friends about what happened (and, if you can, to your parents) especially if you're feeling shaky or upset. The sooner you talk about it, the sooner you can start to feel better and put the whole thing behind you.

THEFT

"It was really hot at the concert, so I put my jacket under the seat. I kept turning around to check that it was okay. Then one minute it was there, and the next time I turned around, it was gone. It ruined my whole night. My dad bought me a new one, but that didn't really make me feel much better. I just got really choked up every time I thought about my jacket, which I'd really loved, belonging to someone else who was horrible enough to steal it. I know jackets don't have feelings and that it sounds really babyish, but I couldn't help it."

Marisa, 14

"Our house got burgled while we were on vacation. Most of the stuff was insured—the television, my stereo, my mom's jewelry—but the house was a real mess. The most disgusting thing was the robber went to the bathroom and wiped his butt on one of our towels! All my friends thought that was really funny, and I could really have used their support, not laughter, because the whole thing was the worst thing that ever happened to me. It made me feel sick, knowing a stranger had been in my room

and gone through my things. I felt like it wasn't my room anymore, and I couldn't bear to sleep in there. I slept in my brother's room instead. When the insurance money came through, my mom and dad let me redecorate my room, and it was okay after that. It was like getting rid of the ghost of the burglar by throwing out everything he'd touched."

Caroline, 15

Being a victim of theft—from having your pocket picked to discovering that your home has been broken into—can be more disturbing than you can imagine, if you've never been there yourself. Beyond the sadness of losing something you liked, there's a horrible, horrible feeling of being violated.

Obviously, you should always report a theft—there's always a chance that the thief might get caught (which would be satisfying) and that you might even get your possessions back (which would be nicer still). Less obviously, it's also important to make sure you talk your feelings through with someone you're close to. Whereas, if you'd been flashed or attacked, people around you would realize right away that you needed their support in order to get back on your feet, they may not figure out right away that their backup is needed—so don't be afraid to let them know that it is.

MUGGING

"My mom got mugged as she was getting out of her car, even though the street was really busy. One man grabbed her bag, and the other ripped her watch off her wrist, and then they both ran away. She said she couldn't

believe how quickly it happened, but apart from a big scratch on her wrist where they pulled her watch off, she wasn't hurt. I suppose it could have been a lot worse."

Andie, 17

"A boy in my cousin's school got beaten up for his sneakers by some boys from another school. He got a black eye and a broken nose. If I was him, I think I'd have just given them the sneakers right away—I mean, it's only a pair of shoes, isn't it?"

Alan, 16

Being mugged means getting attacked, and usually having something stolen from you at the same time, but "mugging" is a pretty general word, and people use it to refer to a number of very different situations. For instance, some muggings involve just one person, some involve many. Sometimes the attacker or attackers have a weapon and sometimes they don't. On one end of the scale, a mugger can just turn up, grab something off their victim and dash off, or they can act threatening and then dash off as soon as they've gotten what they want. On the other end of the scale, muggings can be very violent crimes indeed. Victims can be pushed around, punched, kicked, or attacked with a weapon—maybe because they are reluctant to hand over their stuff, but sometimes, unfortunately, just because the mugger is dangerous, violent, and unstable.

Luckily, muggings rarely happen in busy or well-lit places, so with a few precautions, there's no reason why you should ever have this horrible trauma happen to you. It's always worth knowing, however, exactly what to do if you are attacked, just in case:

• If someone grabs something of yours from you, your natural instinct is probably to try and get it back. But unless you think you can snatch it off them and still get away in double-quick time, you should just run. At least that way you can get help from others and you don't run the risk of getting hurt.

• If someone grabs or threatens you, asking for your money, the most important thing to keep in mind is getting away. If you think you can flee safely, make a break for it.

• If you can't run, your next step is to make as much noise as possible—shout, scream, and/or set off your personal alarm. A jumpy mugger might be shocked enough, or worried enough about attracting attention to give up and get lost, or at least hesitate for long enough for you to make a break for it.

• If you can't get away immediately, bear in mind that the mugger is probably just after your money, and not planning to hurt you. So shove your bag, money, or whatever else the mugger seems to be after in their direction, and then scatter—as fast as you can. Remember: Your safety is *way* more important than any material possession. *Things* can be replaced. *You* can't.

• If escape isn't possible (a mugger won't let you go even after they've robbed you, and you've made as much noise as possible) your only option is to get physical in self-defense. See the section called *Fighting Back*, further on.

If you're mugged, it's essential to report it to the police, and equally essential to get some emotional help—from friends, family, and maybe even from a trained counselor so that you can get back on your feet and get on with your life and sleep soundly without feeling traumatized and frightened by what's happened.

RAPE AND SEXUAL ASSAULT

"My aunt got sexually assaulted. It was in the park, and it was broad daylight. I think the guy hurt her quite badly, too, because she was in the hospital—I didn't go, but my dad went to visit her and when he came back he was crying. No one would tell me much else about it. I don't think they ever caught him."

Lucie, 14

"I was raped by my mom's boyfriend. The worst thing was that he'd always been nice to me before that, and I quite liked him. He didn't hurt me, but it was horrible. I don't think anyone could imagine just how disgusting it was. I never reported it, because I didn't think anyone would believe me—especially my mom. It happened four years ago, and it's only now that I'm starting to feel alright about boys getting anywhere near me—before that I couldn't even bear the thought of someone touching me. I think that's what I'm the most angry about now: all those years when my friends were dating and having fun... It's like he stole part of my life from me."

Geraldine, 20

Sexual assault is any kind of attack where there is a sexual angle—in other words, the attacker touches, grabs, or injures their victim's private parts or breasts, forces their victim to perform some kind of sexual act, or attempts to rape their victim. Rape, in case you aren't clear about this, is where an attacker forces the victim to have sexual intercourse against their will.

We often automatically think of a rapist as some sicko who lurks in bushes, but in fact, most rapes are committed by someone the victim knows—someone the victim probably thought was perfectly friendly, nice, normal, and trustworthy. We looked at date rape back in Chapter Two, but sometimes girls and women are raped by people they know but have never dated or been at all intimate with. This is sometimes called *acquaintance rape*, and like date rape, it's no less vile or serious than being raped by a stranger. These rapes often take place in situations where the victim fully—and rightfully—expected to be safe.

Of course, sometimes a rapist *is* a sick stranger, waiting around for an opportunity to strike. Like any attacker, rapists generally avoid busy or well-lit areas—yet another good reason to take precautions and avoid risky situations. But how do you avoid a potential acquaintance rapist? It would be terrible to go through life not feeling safe anywhere, with anyone, but it's always worth being a little cautious and trusting your instincts when you feel uncomfortable around someone. If you get a funny feeling about someone you know—a family friend perhaps, a relative, *anyone*—you should always do your best to avoid being alone with them. If they come on to you, touch or brush up against you or make creepy remarks, take it as a danger signal and be doubly careful.

If you ever find yourself in a situation, whether it's with a stranger or with someone you know, where you suspect that you're in danger of being raped, you should:

• Make it clear that you don't want to have sex. Shout "No!" or whatever else comes into your head, and push the attacker away.

• Make plenty of noise—it could put the attacker off or alert someone else to what's going on.

• Try other tactics to put the attacker off: tell him you've got your period, tell him you've got a sexually transmitted disease or AIDS, tell him you're pregnant, tell him you're going to be sick and then make vomity noises, cry, swear and curse unstoppably, laugh, spit, blow snot out of your nose, wet yourself.

• If you know the attacker, you could try to reason with him. You could tell him that you're sure he's a nice guy, deep down, and he's going to feel dreadful about this afterward. Or ask him to imagine how he'd feel if his girlfriend, mom, or sister was raped.

• Think carefully before you try to defend yourself physically. If a rapist is violent, or has a weapon, you could end up getting hurt more badly than you would have if you hadn't fought back. However, hurting your attacker or using all your strength to struggle *could* give you the vital chance to get away. If you decide to get physical, follow the guidelines in the section called *Fighting Back*, on page 129.

If you are assaulted or raped, you need to get help. If you're badly injured, you'll need to get to a hospital, where the doctors and nurses will look after you, and will also inform the police, who'll come by and see you.

Don't be afraid to call 911 and ask for an ambulance, if you're not sure where the nearest hospital is or unsure of how you'll be able to get there.

Even if you don't need medical help, you'll definitely need emotional support. Some women and girls feel so shocked after this kind of experience that they feel they don't actually want to tell anyone what has happened, but it's essential that you don't suffer alone. All sexual attacks should be reported to the police, but you'll most likely want some comfort and backup from someone you know first. Ideally, you should talk to your parents, close friends, and/or anyone else you trust—a relative, a teacher, whoever. You could also call the Rape Crisis line (see *Where to Get Help* at the back of this book), which is manned by sympathetic, trained counselors who are incredibly easy to talk to and will be totally understanding.

When you report a rape or assault to the police, they'll want you to get down to the nearest police station right away, and can pick you up if you can't get there by yourself. Although you'll probably feel desperate to have a shower or bath, and change into clean clothes before you do anything else, it's very important that you don't because it would mean washing away vital evidence. At the police station, you'll be looked after by a female officer, who will take down details of what happened. A police doctor will deal with any injuries you have as well as taking samples of anything that could be used as evidence (like semen, or, if you scratched your attacker, skin from under your fingernails). Once you're finished at the station, the police will make arrangements for you to get home safely.

If you're of two minds about reporting the attack to the police, it's worth knowing that you'll be doing a very good, very important thing if you can gather up the courage to go through with it. First, if you bring your attacker to justice, it might save other girls and women from going through what you've been through. Second, many men are very cocky about their chances of getting away with rape and assault, because they think that their victims will be too scared or embarrassed to go to the police. If you prove them wrong, you certainly burst *their* bubble—and maybe take a chunk out of other potential rapists' confidence too.

ABDUCTION

Abduction literally means being taken away—sort of like being kidnapped, but without the ransom demand. This kind of crime is incredibly scary but, thank goodness, very rare. Abductors usually strike in quiet areas, lonely places, and empty buildings and often rely on their cars to make a getaway with their victims.

If the unthinkable ever happened, and you are grabbed by someone, you should always:

- Try to get away immediately.

- Shout, scream, set off your personal alarm.

- Yell someone's name—any name that comes into your head, but ideally a boy's name—as if there is someone with you or nearby that the abductor hasn't seen.

- Use physical force. (See *Fighting Back* on page 129.)

If none of the above works, and an abductor is able to get you into his car, or take you somewhere else, you should:

• Tell the abductor that someone knows exactly where you were going and how you were getting there, and will be looking for you at this very moment.

• Stay calm and talk to the abductor as much as you can. Try to be friendly and keep him calm, and repeatedly tell him your name and as much as possible about your family and your life. Unlike an attacker who attacks suddenly and violently, an abductor has time to think—and if you could make him get to know you, it would be much harder for him to hurt you. It might also make it possible to reason with the abductor.

FIGHTING BACK

Defending yourself

Let's face it—if you were attacked, you would almost certainly be at a physical disadvantage. Your attacker would probably be stronger and bigger than you. He might have a weapon or one or more other people with him. You would be shocked and surprised at having been attacked, while he would have had a chance to think about it. You probably almost never get physical while he is likely to get in a lot of practice. In other words, it's a major mismatch, and you are not going to suddenly turn into some hero from a movie and punch his lights out, so if you had visions of yourself standing proudly with one foot on your unconscious attacker as a police car roars up and a crowd gathers around applauding wildly, forget it. The key to using physical force successfully is to try and inflict a small but painful injury which will stun your attacker for long enough to give you a chance to get away. In other words, getting away is still your number one priority. Here are some tips on getting rough.

• Even certified weaklings can do some damage when there is anger behind their actions. Without taking too much time about it, gather together all your feelings of anger at this person who has encroached on your freedom and your body and ruined your day. Think: How *dare* he! Then strike, putting all that anger into what you do.

• Aim for tender areas where your strike will have the maximum effect. The prime spots are:
- the knee cap (kick it);
- the shins (kick them);
- the testicles/balls/whatever you want to call them (kick, punch, crush, squeeze, or grab and twist them);
- the little finger (shove it backward);
- the throat (squeeze the windpipe, punch, or—if possible —kick, aiming for the Adam's apple);
- the eye (poke your finger sharply into it);
- the nose (aim to get the palm of your hand flat underneath it and shove upward for all you're worth, as if you were trying to push the whole nose upward and back into the attacker's face).

• When kicking or punching, try to put all your physical weight behind you, and all the force you can into doing it.

• Don't forget about biting. Even the weakest person can manage a very effective chomp that will be incredibly painful and surprising.

• Whatever method of attack you use, it's always best to try just one, and then use the seconds afterward to try and get away. Don't wait and see what effect you've had, or stop to have one more try—wriggle free and run. Only strike again if you've failed to get away the first time.

Defending other people

If you see someone else being attacked, it's never a good idea to jump in, at the risk of getting hurt yourself. However, you should obviously never ignore it, either—imagine yourself in the position of the victim and how dismayed and horrified you'd be to see people walking past instead of helping you. If you see an attack of any kind happening, you should:

• Shout for help or set off your personal alarm to attract other people's attention.

• If there are other people around, grab them and encourage them to help. If not, run to the nearest busy place to get assistance.

• Once someone else is involved, or if there's no one else around, go and phone the police.

Chapter 8 Confidence Builders

Sometimes it seems that bad news is everywhere. Watching the news, reading the papers, and talking to other people you often hear so much nasty stuff about crime that you can end up feeling quite depressed and frightened.

The most important thing to remember is that bad news is usually the only news we get to hear. Although every day any number of people will have bad things happen to them, many of which we'll get to hear about, we won't get to hear about the millions and millions and millions of others who have gone to bed having had yet another perfectly ordinary, happy, safe 24 hours. Let's face it—we're never going to switch on the news and hear the newscaster saying: "And today, a fourteen-year-old girl from New York got up, ate some cornflakes, took the bus to school, and hung around a shopping center with her friends afterward before catching the bus and arriving home in time for dinner. Later on we'll be bringing you the full report on the student who went on a blind date that turned out to be a lot of fun, but now it's over to Carol for today's financial report."

Yes, yes, I know it's an obvious point to make, but it's something we can often forget, and it's important that we don't go through life feeling convinced that the world is a terrible, horrible place and that bad things are just waiting to happen to us. That feeling is sometimes known as "victim mentality," and it's often been suggested that people who think that way actually have a higher chance of having bad things happen to them in the first place. It's certainly true that an attacker is more likely to zero in on people who look like they lack confidence and seem unsure—that's been proven in tests where convicted muggers and rapists have been shown videos of all sorts of different people walking down the street, and asked which ones they'd be most likely to attack.

While it's important that you don't go through life with victim mentality, it's equally important not to have "false confidence." Feelings of being invincible or lucky and somehow believing that nothing bad could ever possibly happen to you is even more dangerous, because you could end up striding blithely into hazardous situations and deliberately ignoring your instincts.

Being confident is a good thing, but that doesn't mean that being scared is a bad thing. When you feel edgy, nervous, or just plain frightened, it's a warning signal from your brain, and it can pay to think of these instincts as your sixth sense. If you ignore them and tell yourself that you're just being silly and should pull yourself together, you could end up getting in deeper trouble. Fear is good when you use it in the right way: Take it as your cue to get out of the situation as swiftly as possible.

But let's get back to talking about confidence. There's no doubt, that confidence and a positive frame of mind are important when it comes to keeping yourself safe. Let's check out the other ways you can give your confidence levels a jump start.

LOOKING CONFIDENT

Body language really is amazing. When your body language says that you are confident, it does two things. First, it sends out the right signals to other people—that you know what you're up to, you want to be left alone, and you're not vulnerable. Second, it works almost like magic in making you *feel* instantly more confident, even if you weren't feeling that way to begin with. Here's how to say "I'm confident" in body language.

• Walk briskly and purposefully, like you know where you're going (even if you don't!).

• Walk tall, with your shoulders back and your head up—don't hunch over, slouch, or stare at the ground.

• Try to keep your feet slightly apart when you walk to be sure of getting a good balance—it'll make your way of walking look that much more confident, and help you walk tall.

• Let your arms swing in a relaxed way by your sides. Don't stuff your hands in your pockets (if it's cold, get a pair of gloves!) or fold your arms across your chest.

• Don't keep looking behind you, as if you're *expecting* to be followed.

• If you're feeling nervous or uptight, take a deep breath in, then a long breath out, out loud. This relaxes your muscles and helps get rid of tension.

TAKING SELF-DEFENSE CLASSES

Many people find that knowing a bit about self-defense makes them feel safer and more confident. And, of course, knowing self-defense techniques can also give you a better chance of defending yourself physically if the worst ever came to the worst. However, self-defense needs to be very well taught—in a class by a top-notch teacher, ideally. Videos can be good, but are not as effective as a class, where a teacher can tell you if you're doing things wrong, and reading a book on the subject certainly isn't going to be good enough at all. It's also important not to become falsely confident after learning about self-defense, and assume that you can now do whatever you want, whenever, wherever, without a care in the world. You've got to realize that self-defense has it's limitations—if you were attacked by someone with a weapon, or by more than one person, you'd suddenly be looking at a completely different ball game. And if you've got visions of yourself springing around like a Power Ranger, arms and legs flailing as one baddie after another bites the dust, it's time for a reality check. Fact is, even if your fighting skills made Jean Claude Van Damme look like Mr. Rogers, your first choice of action, if you were attacked, should still be to try and run away to safety. Failing that, you would use the things you had learned to incapacitate your attacker for long enough to give you a chance to get away—that's the whole idea of self-defense.

It's worth bearing in mind that *any* kind of exercise or sport you do will help build up your strength, stamina, posture, and confidence—all of which are very useful when it comes to self-protection.

OWNING A PERSONAL ALARM

A personal alarm is a little gadget, sometimes called a rape alarm, which is small enough to fit into a bag or pocket. They're easy to use: When you feel that you're in danger, you just activate them with the push of a button, and they let out an ear-piercing, shrieking noise. This alone is often enough to scare an attacker off. Failing that, it can startle them for long enough to give you a chance to get away. It also attracts the attention of other people around who can come to your rescue, and lets passersby know that they're witnessing a serious situation in which their help is needed.

Personal alarms are not expensive, and are well worth the investment. You can buy them from many different stores, or by mail order.

A personal alarm is the best thing you can carry with you to boost your confidence and use to protect yourself (although, of course, it would be silly to assume that you can take risks just because you have one with you). Carrying something else that you can actually use to defend yourself can seem like a good idea, but by and large, it's not, for many reasons. For instance:

- It's illegal to carry what the police call an "offensive weapon"—that covers guns and knives of any sort (except small penknives and Swiss army knives), brass knuckles, and any other thing that is obviously intended for use as a weapon (i.e., a billiard ball in a sock—although billiard balls and socks are not weapons, there's no other reason why you'd be carrying one inside the other). You can also get into trouble for carrying anything that you could use to harm someone if the police think that that's why you're carrying it—that goes for hammers, meat cleavers, and anything else that you probably wouldn't be hauling around with you for any other reason.

• If you carry a weapon, an attacker could grab it and use it to hurt *you* instead—in other words, you could put yourself in more danger than you'd have been in if you hadn't had the weapon in the first place.

• Producing a weapon can also scare an attacker into hurting you "in self-defense"—if they think there's a chance you could hurt them badly with your weapon, they'll want to make sure that doesn't happen—and that doesn't necessarily mean that they'll run away, especially if they think that they're stronger than you, or more skillful at using a weapon.

Considering all that, it's clear that carrying a weapon is a bad idea, even if it makes you feel safer. If you feel driven to carry something you can use to protect yourself physically, go for a heavy umbrella (which you could use to defend yourself) or a perfume, spray deodorant, or hair spray (which you could spray in someone's eyes).

All of the above can certainly help in making you feel more at ease, and could even make an actual difference in a bad situation. But without a doubt, the best confidence booster of all is knowledge. The more you know about being prepared, avoiding risks, and every other aspect of personal protection, the happier and safer you're going to feel. In other words, just by making it through to here, the end of this book, you've done yourself the biggest favor of all.

Where To Get Help

FINDING SOMEONE TO TALK TO RIGHT AWAY

If you'd like to talk to a friendly, helpful, trained counselor about any problem—including abuse, bullying, or being the victim of a crime—you can call any of these three wonderful organizations:

Family Service America (800) 221-2681

Lines are open during business hours and they can direct you to local agencies. Calls are free nationwide.

Youth Crisis and Runaway Hotline (800) 448-4663

Lines are open 24 hours a day, every day, and calls are free nationwide.

Parents Anonymous/Family Hotline (800) 843-5437

Lines are open 24 hours a day, every day, and calls are free nationwide.

You can also find many useful numbers in your local phone book, including the Rape Crisis Center, for victims of rape and sexual assault. You'll find it under "R."

FINDING A COUNSELOR

If you think you'd like to talk to a counselor face to face, your school or family doctor should be able to put you in contact with one.

Index